CREATING THE AMERICAN PRESIDENCY 1775-1789

William B. Michaelsen

Pace University

UNIVERSITY PRESS OF AMERICA

LANHAM • NEW YORK • LONDON

Library of Congress Cataloging in Publication Data

Michaelsen, William B., 1914-
    Creating the American presidency, 1775-1789.

    Bibliography: p.
    Includes index.
    1. Presidents—United States—History.   2. Executive
power—United States—History.   3. United States.
Constitutional Convention (1787)   I. Title.
JK511.M53   1987   353.03'1'09   86-28086
ISBN 0-8191-5806-2 (alk. paper)
ISBN 0-8191-5807-0 (pbk. : alk. paper)

For Mary

Who Made It Happen

ACKNOWLEDGMENTS

I acknowledge with thanks the many helpful suggestions made by my students at Pace University, especially their stress on the need for a topical presentation of the constitutional debates.

The librarians at the New York Historical Society Library, the New York Public Library, Bobst Library of New York University, and the Mortola Library at Pace University, Pleasantville, were all very helpful, and I take this opportunity to thank them for their courteous attention to my many requests for assistance.

Part of the manuscript was read by Jane Reynolds Fennelly. I appreciate the suggestions she made, all of which have been incorporated in the book.

I am most indebted to Dr. James Holmes, Professor of History, and Chairman of the History Department at Pace University, as well as my friend, colleague, advisor, and mentor, who very kindly offered to edit the manuscript. I apologize for encroaching on his very busy life. I thank him for his many suggestions, for his demonstrated interest in my work, his encouragement, and his constant willingness to be of help. If this study is a worthwhile contribution, much of the credit should go to Jim Holmes. I hasten to add, however, that I am fully responsible for any errors.

Finally, the book could not have been written without the essential help of my wife, companion, and friend, Mary Michaelsen, who was always available to listen to my thoughts on the subject, and whose tact-

v

ful criticism many times steered me away from difficulties. The dedication of this book to her is just
a very small way of acknowledging her great contribution.

TABLE OF CONTENTS

PREFACE

This is a book on the evolution of executive power during the years 1775 to 1789 and how it led to the creation of the American Presidency. The study was prompted by the interest evinced by students in courses on the Presidency that I have taught over the past ten years, and the lack of an available monograph on this important subject.

The only full-scale treatment of the beginnings of the Presidency is the seminal work of Charles E. Thach, Jr., <u>The Creation of the Presidency</u> - <u>1775-1789</u>, published by Johns Hopkins Press in 1923. It was reprinted in 1969 and is presently out of print.

My intent, therefore, is to fill this void in the study of the Presidency by presenting an account of the American experiences which contributed to the establishment of this most innovative part of our Constitution.

The book is divided into two parts in order to differentiate between the origins of the office at the state level and within the Confederation, and the establishment of the Presidency at the Constitutional Convention.

Part One, consisting of two chapters, is titled "The Executive in a Republican Polity". Chapter One examines the political climate existing at the time of the adoption of the first state constitutions and the effect that it had on the executive office instituted in the states. I trace the change in political thought that occurred respecting executive power, brought on by the exigencies of the Revolutionary War, and the exceptional performance of outstanding state governors working under severe constitutional limitations and restrictions. I examine, also, the effect that "unbridled legislatures" had on that change. Finally, I analyze the contribution of state experience and state constitutions to the development of the Presidency.

Chapter Two deals with the executive in the Continental Congress and the Confederation. The focus is on the lack of a viable executive structure. The study examines the attempt to perform executive functions through the use of committees, boards, and departments and analyzes the effect of the Confederation experience on the Presidency.

Part Two, consists of three chapters, and is titled "The Constitutional Executive." It covers the period of the Constitutional Convention, the ratification of the Constitution, and the inauguration of George Washington as first President.

Chapter Three is a survey of the Convention and the manner in which it operated, with the emphasis placed on the executive article. The executive provisions in the three main plans of government are detailed, as is the work of the three major committees. There is a short analysis of the contributions of those Framers who were most responsible for the creation of the Presidency. Finally, the influence of George Washington on the establishment of the Presidency is examined.

Chapter Four is the heart of the study. It deals with the debates at the Constitutional Convention. I present the debates on the Presidency in topical form.

Preface

This is a departure from the usual chronological
treatment and is patterned after Saul Padovar's, <u>To
Secure</u> <u>These</u> <u>Blessings:</u> <u>Great</u> <u>Debates</u> <u>of</u> <u>the</u> <u>Constitu-
tion</u> (New York 1962). The source used is Madison's
<u>Notes</u>, as edited by Max Farrand. I have extracted from
those notes the discussions pertaining to the Presidency and have presented them as twelve separate debates. Those debates are the best source of information we have on the political thinking and reasoning
of the Framers in their pursuit of a viable executive
structure within a republican polity. Presenting them
in topical form enables the reader to better follow
these important discussions and to appreciate and
evaluate the many factors affecting the creation of
the office. The "intent of the Framers" can be best
examined through the topical format.

Madison recorded the remarks of the Framers as
they were made. These were not always prepared
speeches, but mostly extemporaneous presentations.
Consequently, there was much that was repetitive. On
many occasions, also, the speakers would wander from
their subject or address several topics at the same
time. Therefore, in my presentation of the debates, I
report only the most important and cogent arguments,
shunning repetitious remarks, and those not germane to
the debate, but making every effort to preserve intact
the views of the speakers. The debates as presented
are, therefore, not a verbatim rendition of Madison's
<u>Notes</u>, but an edited paraphrased version.

The last chapter deals with the ratification
period and how the Presidency was viewed by Federalists and Antifederalists in the great newspaper and
pamphlet debates, as well as at the ratifying conventions. The book concludes with the election and inauguration of President Washington.

INTRODUCTION

It has been said that America's greatest contribution to the art of government is the American
Presidency. It is a unique office peculiarly American
in origin. It was conceived, invented, and created at
the Constitutional Convention in Philadelphia in 1787
and it is the most innovative part of the constitution.

The purpose of this study is to trace the development of executive power and authority which led
to the creation of the Presidency.

There have been several theories advanced re-
garding the origins of the American Presidency. Some
have contended that the office is a direct descendent
of the English Kings -- an elective monarchy without
kingly trappings and prerogatives.[1] One scholar recently wrote that the office was the consequence of an
evolutionary process which can be traced back to
Jamestown.[2] This view is supported by Joseph E.
Kellenbach, whose study of the Presidency and the
state governors concludes that theirs was a common
origin which "runs back to the kingship through an
ancestral tree nurtured in America." Kellenbach holds
that the Presidency is "the product of an evolutionary
process that began with the founding of the first
English colonies in America."[3] The foremost authority
on the creation of the American Presidency, Charles E.
Thach, Jr., wrote in his seminal work in 1923 that
"The state legislatures' excesses and the incompetency
of Congress as an administrative body produced the

Introduction

presidency."[4]

While acknowledging the merit of the assessments of a long process of executive development in America, this study will focus on a more proximate origin -- the period of constitutional development in America between 1775 and 1789. As for Thach's conclusion on the origins of the Presidency, research shows that such excesses did indeed exist and were of great influence. There is, however, a more positive reason for the changing political thought respecting the executive in America, and that was the outstanding performance of state executives during the period, as well as the effectiveness of the departments established by Congress. This, despite the limitations placed on executives during the early period of constitution-making due in great part to the republican polity of the day.

That polity was widespread. Among its tenets was the insistence that the people would be best served by a strong legislature composed of popularly elected representatives -- mirror images of the people. The power of government was to reside in the legislature. An executive was considered to be nothing more than an adjunct of the legislature -- controlled by it and doing its bidding. Roger Sherman of Connecticut typified the attitude toward the executive. He considered the office "as nothing more than an institution for carrying the will of the legislature into effect."[5]

There was also fear and distrust of executive power. The deteriorating relationship between the colonists and England since 1763 was equated with maladministration in England and also by the colonial governors. Whether or not this actually was the case is not within the scope of this study, but American attitudes toward executive power were much influenced and shaped by their colonial experience, and by the adversarial relationship that existed between the legislature and the governor. This is evident in the

xiv

composition of the executive under the new state constitutions adopted in 1776 and early 1777.

The executive under these early constitutions was
"nothing more than an institution carrying out the
will of the legislature." With few exceptions, the
executive was not given any powers normally associated
with that function. He was to be the administrator of
government and what powers were granted to him were
administrative in nature. He was generally provided
with a Council, usually composed of members of the
legislature, and he could not act without their consent.[6] Governor Edmund Randolph of Virginia considered
himself to be merely a part of the executive council.[7]
There were no executive prerogatives. Since the
legislature was supreme, the executive was not provided with any means of checking that body.

This brought on the legislative excesses mentioned by Thach. It led to the formation of new
opposition factions, or the strengthening of older
ones, intent on providing a properly balanced, more
equitable system of government.

Experienced politicians recognized the inadequacies of the executive under the new constitutions.
Those opposed to legislative omnipotence supported
strengthening the power of the executive to provide a
check against precipitate and unjust legislation.
This is especially evident in Pennsylvania, where a
strong anti-constitutional party was formed, aimed at
amending the old constitution or adopting a new one.
Strengthening the executive was one of the reforms
advocated.

The experience in Pennsylvania, and in other
states, materially influenced constitution-making in
New York. The New York constitution was adopted in
June, 1777 after all the other states except Massachusetts had acted. The first real changes in republican
polity are seen in the New York constitution. The

Introduction

most important of these related to the executive. The
New York governor was more than just an administrator
or a creature of the legislature. He derived his
power from the people through a popular election. He
had powers under the constitution which enabled him to
review legislation. Through the veto power he was
able to check legislative excesses. Through the appointive power the governor could staff his administration with his own supporters. These were not absolute powers -- they were shared with councils appointed for the purpose -- but the New York governorship
was a definite departure from the weak executive
structure of other states.

The adoption of the New York constitution heralds
the beginning of the change in political thinking with
respect to executive power. Much of this change was
brought on by the poor experience in other states, but
war-time conditions in New York also contributed to
it. New York was the main battle ground of the American Revolution beginning in the summer of 1776 and
into 1777. New York City fell to the British and
continued to be occupied by them until the end of the
war. The exigencies of war pointed up the necessity
of a strong executive to act as commander in chief of
state forces. Because the legislature could not meet
continuously, the governor was given greater statutory
authority to help in governing the state. Gradually,
leadership of the state was equated with the governorship.

The Revolution brought on similar changes in executive function in the other states. No changes were
made in the constitutional structure of the office,
but, as a practical matter, greater authority was
granted the executives by the legislatures. The
governor of the state became the avowed leader and the
focus of attention. The leading politicians of each
state were attracted to the office. The war governors
performed their role in an exceptional manner and
this, of course, contributed to the continuing change

in perception of the role of the executive in government.[8]

The change occurred more slowly in the government
of the Continental Congress and of the Confederation.
No executive was provided for the federal government.
The President of Congress was merely the presiding
officer of congressional meetings. He was still a
delegate from his state, participating in debate, and
casting his vote. He had no executive or administrative powers. Gradually, however, out of necessity, he
became the acknowledged administrator of the government and the representative of Congress. He corres-
ponded with the governors of the states and with
George Washington as commander in chief. He was considered the titular head of government although this
carried no important powers. The actual executive
function was carried on by legislative committees
within Congress. These soon became standing committees headed by chairmen who, by default, performed
executive duties. Responsibility for execution, however, was always exclusively in the hands of Congress.
Obviously, this was cumbersome and inefficient, and
there was much criticism of the practice in and out of
Congress. The chaos generated by a legislature attempting to "play the executive"[9] eventually led to the
formation of executive departments headed by nonmembers of Congress who were granted a greater degree
of authority. The performance of these department
heads contributed immensely to the perception of the
need for strength, unity, and independence in the executive.[10]

The change in the concept of executive power
reached its climax at the Constitutional Convention in
1787. The Convention was dominated by a nationalist
faction desirous of a strong central government. It
consisted of politicians who had served in state governments and in the Confederation and were fully aware
of the need for executive strength and independence.
They recognized the executive as a vital part of

government playing a coordinate role with the legislature and judiciary. The debates at the Convention on the executive reflect those perceptions.

As a consequence of the efforts of these politicians the Presidency was created. The powers and duties assigned to the office came primarily from the constitutions of New York and Massachusetts. The strong Presidency that emerged was the product of the changing political perception of executive power which evolved during the formative years of American government at the federal and state levels.

CREATING THE AMERICAN PRESIDENCY 1775-1789

PART I

The Executive in a Republican Polity

1

CHAPTER ONE

The State Executives

The American Presidency was the product of American experience, particularly between 1775 and 1787, during which time a change in the concept of the executive as part of government occurred. At the beginning of the period the executive was viewed with suspicion and fear, but by the end Americans had grown to accept the executive as an essential part of government and "emphatically the Representative of the whole people at large," as the Address of the Massachusetts Convention expressed it in March, 1780.[1] Among the factors contributing to the acceptance of the executive, and the eventual enlargement of executive power, was the failure of state constitutions to provide a sufficient check on the legislature. The change was also influenced by the greater effectiveness of the state governors and the heads of departments during the Confederation. In order to better understand the impact that this experience had on the creation of the Presidency, it is necessary to consider the polity that existed both at the state and Confederation level and to consider the changes during the period. Those changes included the constitutional and political development of the executive office.

It would have been virtually impossible in 1775 to have deliberately created the strong Presidency, or to have established the limited form of government with its necessary checks and balances, that emerged from the Constitutional Convention. The concept of republicanism as perceived by the American of that day was too much influenced by his recent experience with colonial governors and by his perception, exaggerated though it may have been, of the tyranny of the King of England. In 1776 the American people were convinced, along with Thomas Paine, that "the nearer any government approaches to a republic, the less business there is for a king."[2] This view of the strong executive resulted in the creation of weak state executives under the new constitutions. It also contributed to the failure to provide for a national executive in the Articles of Confederation. Thomas Jefferson recognized this tendency when he wrote:

> Before the Revolution we were all good
> English Whigs, cordial in their free
> principles, and in their jealousies of
> their executive Magistrates. These
> jealousies are apparent in all our state
> constitutions.[3]

Several towns in Massachusetts considered an executive "needless in a free state" and "dangerous to the liberty of the people."[4]

The new state governments were essentially creations of this Whig philosophy. It was a philosophy that had been practiced by Americans over the course of years as they battled the colonial governors. The adversarial relationship between the assemblies and the governors persisted throughout the colonial period and intensified during the last years of British rule. The philosophy was based on the assumption by the assemblies that liberty could best be safeguarded when the real power in government was in the hands of the people through their representatives. Benjamin Church echoed this sentiment on March 5, 1773:

> The liberty of the people is exactly
> proportional to the share the body of
> the people have in the legislature, and

> the check placed by the constitution on
> the executive power.[5]

The consequence of the confrontation between the legislature and the executive led to an erosion in the power of the colonial governor and his greater dependence on the legislature. Sir James Wright, for sixteen years Royal Governor of Georgia, complained to London that "the whole executive power is assumed by them [the Provincial Congress] and the King's government remains little else than nominally so."[6] This distrust of executive power and the concomitant reliance of Americans on their own legislatures as mirror images of themselves was deemed essential to a republic and was clearly manifested in the early state constitutions. The state executive in all the new constitutions, except those of New York and Massachusetts, was constituted as a subordinate branch of government while the legislature had the supreme power.

The new state governments represented the first successful efforts to form republican governments on the basis of written constitutions,[7] and, as Jefferson indicated, were essentially creations of the Whig philosophy that dominated American political thinking. The colonists had long supported the English Whigs and this was especially true after 1763 when there was a noticeable deterioration in the relationship between England and her colonies. More and more Americans considered themselves to be Whigs. The colonists were steeped in English history and government and agreed with such philosophers as Montesquieu that the English Whig constitution was the best contrived by man. They became convinced that this constitution was being perverted and in the end "they revolted not against the English constitution but on behalf of it," and "an uncorrupted English constitution remained for most Americans the model of what a constitution should be."[8]

This is the model which Americans attempted to

apply to their own state constitutions during that remarkable spate of constitution-making which took place literally "in the midst of a revolution."[9] In 1776 eight of the original thirteen states formed new governments. Connecticut and Rhode Island, the charter colonies, amended their former liberal charter governments to the new conditions of sovereignty. Georgia and New York adopted new constitutions in 1777; Massachusetts, in 1780.

But since the spectrum of American Whiggery ranged from conservatives to radicals and included a large number of moderates,[10] the new constitutions in fact reflected the philosophy of the faction that dominated a particular state. Thus, we see some state constitutions where the so-called "democratic" element predominated, and others more conservative, adhering closer to the former colonial governments. There were some obvious points of agreement between factions, among which was the conviction that to ensure liberty required the participation of the people in government. The extent of popular participation and the method of checking the executive marked the real difference between the points of view.

Essentially the general struggle between radicals and conservatives within each state molded the state constitutions. Conservative Whigs, usually represented by the more affluent in the community and seeking stability in government, were more inclined to retain the familiar colonial structure of government in which the strong executive was assisted by an appointed Council representing the large landed and commercial interests, with a popularly elected house.

Radical Whigs, on the other hand, consisting increasingly of a new breed in politics -- mechanics, artisans, young lawyers, and back-country men of all classes -- were suspicious of executive power. They placed their confidence in strong legislatures, preferably unicameral. They insisted, in any case, even where two houses were involved, that both be representative of the people at large. The legislature would perform the functions of legislation and discharge the duties of execution as well. Thus the liberties of the people would be well guarded.

The moderate wing could not accept the extremism of the radicals and was more inclined to side with the conservatives in any confrontation between the two factions.[11] The compromises which took place during the process of constitution-making, therefore, were defined by the attempt to mold a conservative-moderate consensus. This consensus was achieved in most of the new states. The conservatives prevailed in establishing bicameral legislatures in all states except Pennsylvania, Georgia, and New Hampshire. The conservatives had to concede defeat in their desire for strong executives, but they succeeded in establishing executive departments in every state. These consisted of one-man executives, although in most states the executive was little more than an administrator or presiding officer of an executive council. This attitude reflected Jefferson's plan of government for Virginia, which specifically called for an "Administrator."[12] This was the extent of the conservatives' accomplishments in constitution-making during this period. The executive office, deemed essential in government and retained in the state constitutions, was nevertheless the product of public antipathy toward strong executive power; in its weakened form, it did not provide the stability sought by the conservatives, or the check on legislative abuses.

In all of the new constitutions, except those of New York and Massachusetts which were framed at a later date, and in the charter states of Rhode Island and Connecticut, the executive was appointed by the legislature, and, therefore, was the creature of the legislature and dependent upon it for his very existence.[13] Furthermore, his nominal duties were to put into effect the wishes of the legislature and to serve as administrator of government. The executive was a subordinate branch of government while the legislature had the supreme power.

Short executive tenure and provisions for rotation in office were the devices employed in most states to thwart ambitious men from seizing power and establishing themselves as tyrants. The predominant thought was that "where annual elections end, there slavery begins."[14] Maryland's constitution provided:

> A long continuance in the first executive departments of power or trust is dangerous to liberty. A rotation, therefore, in those departments is one of the best securities of permanent freedom.[15]

Hence, a one-year term was provided and, indeed, every state followed suit but three: New York, Delaware, and South Carolina. Furthermore, all of the southern states, together with Pennsylvania, Delaware, and Maryland, limited the number of years that an executive could serve by imposing restrictions on reelection. The most restrictive reelection provision was that of Georgia, which has been characterized by William Webster as "fanaticism . . . carried to the highest degree of absurdity."[16] Georgia restricted its governors to a tenure of only one year out of every three. The result was that during the period from 1776 to 1788, Georgia had fifteen governors whereas all of the other states averaged only four.

The executive was also restrained by limitations on his powers. Those powers nominally placed in the hands of the executive were instead allocated to the legislature or to an executive council. Councils were an outgrowth of colonial government and were included, in one form or another, in every constitution except those of Rhode Island, Connecticut, and New York. New York did not provide for an executive council as such, but instituted a Council of Revision and a Council of

The State Executives

Appointment to restrict the governor in the exercise
of the veto power and the appointive power. Executive
councils were designed to advise the executive and to
control his actions. Councilors were generally members
of the legislature, selected by the legislature.

The important absolute veto power formerly in the
hands of colonial governors as surrogates to the King
of England, was given to the President of the Republic
of South Carolina under its first constitution, but
this power was rescinded after two years because it
was not considered suitable in a republican government. Only New York and Massachusetts provided for a
qualified veto. In Massachusetts the Governor alone
exercised the veto power and his veto could be overridden by a two-thirds vote of both houses of the
legislature. In New York an unusual and controversial
Council of Revision was established with the governor
as a member and empowered to vote in the event of a
tie. The other members of the Council were the
Chancellor and the judges of the Supreme Court. This
Council exercised the veto power, but its veto could
be overridden by a two-thirds vote of the legislature.
There was no revisionary power of any kind in any of
the other states although Georgia provided that its
Executive Council could review all legislative acts.
This was not a veto power but rather a form of judicial review. The governor, who normally presided over
the Council, was not permitted to be present when the
Council reviewed legislation.

The pardoning power was generally placed in the
hands of the executive branch, but it was not necessarily the exclusive preserve of the governor. New
York, Maryland, and South Carolina gave this power to
the governor. Virginia and Georgia retained the pardoning power in the legislative branch, and the other
states granted the power to the governor with the
consent of the executive council.

A particular thorn in the side of the colonists

had been the use of the appointive power by the colonial governors. This had led to the installation of
the notorious "placemen."[17] Therefore, it is not surprising that the power of appointment was jealously
guarded and never wholly given to the executive.
Usually this power was placed jointly in the hands of
the executive and council, with the governor merely an
agent of the council. In Georgia all the officers of
government were elected by the people. In three
states they were chosen by the legislature, and in
four states mainly by the legislature although some
appointments were given to the executive and the council. In New York, appointments were in the hands of a
Council of Appointment consisting of the Governor and
four senators appointed each year by the Assembly. The
authority on the New York Council of Appointment, J.
M. Gitterman, contends that the New York convention
was "unwilling to trust either the Governor, the Senate or the Assembly with the sole appointing power."[18]
The intent in New York was not to reduce the power of
the Governor but to prevent the misuse of power.
Massachusetts was the only state that gave the executive the exclusive nominating authority, although he
did have to seek the advice of his council.

No new state executive was given the prerogative
to dissolve the legislature enjoyed by the colonial
governors. The New York governor had the power to
prorogue, but not for more than 60 days in any year.
In all the states, pre-set times for the legislature
to meet were established either by the constitution,
by statute, or upon adjournment of the legislature and
the executive had no power to prevent that body from
meeting. The executive was given the authority to
call the legislature into special session, and to
determine where the meeting was to take place, but
this was considered more of a wartime measure than a
substantive power.

New York and North Carolina were the only states
which permitted their governor to introduce legisla-

tion. This was somewhat unusual given the general opinion that in a republican polity the executive should not interfere in matters pertaining to the legislature. New York's provision can be understood in the light of the state's reaction against the success of the radicals in neighboring Pennsylvania.[19]

The state constitution-makers held to their own interpretation of the doctrine of separation of powers. They generally adhered to the precept exemplified in the Maryland constitution that "the legislative, executive, and judicial powers of government ought to be forever separate and distinct from each other."[20] But their interpretation of this doctrine was to place all essential powers in the hands of the legislature and provide the executive with only such powers as would permit him to carry out the edicts of the legislature. The executive was obviously hamstrung by the fact that he was appointed by the legislature, had a short one-year term, was restricted insofar as reappointment was concerned, lacked the veto power and, hence, could not check the legislature. In effect he was not an initiator of policy but merely an agent of the legislature in carrying out its policy. The fact that only the legislature could initiate and enact legislation free from countervailing checks meant that it was the legislature which established policy. The doctrine of separation of powers appears to have been aimed at restricting the powers of the executive and preventing him from entering the legislative field.

This was not, however, the case in New York. The greatest contrast between the constitution of New York and that of the other states is this important consideration: the New York executive had a voice-role in policy-making; the executive of the other states did not. The New York executive's power in this respect can be seen in the manner of his election, his three-year term, his unlimited eligibility for reelection, his power to introduce legislation, and especially his veto and appointive powers. Although the veto power

was shared with the Council of Revision, in practice
Governor Clinton was able to dominate the process.
Clinton's dominance of the Council of Appointment, a
legislative-executive mix, also demonstrates his competency and his strength. Clinton was strong enough to
assume the important function of nomination although
nothing in the constitution gave this power specifically to the governor.[21]

The one important area of executive power in
which there was general consensus among the states was
that of commander in chief. Since these early constitutions were framed during a period of war where
invasion of state territory was a definite possibility
and often a reality, there was little objection to
placing powers over the army in the hands of the
executive, but he was to act, true to the temper of
the times, in conjunction with his council. The extent
of the powers of command varied from state to state
depending, to a large extent, as one might expect, on
the proximity of the state to actual fighting. Only
in New York was the governor given full powers as
commander in chief without resort to a council.

It is evident, therefore, that, except for war-
time measures, the executive was stripped of those
prerogative powers formerly associated with the office
and which would enable him to act in the event of
crisis. He was hampered by the provision in every
state except New York, Connecticut, and Rhode Island
that he must act in concert with an executive council.
Governor Edmund Randolph of Virginia, for example,
considered himself only to be "a member of the executive."[22] The obvious intent of the constitution-makers
was to subordinate the executive office to the legislature. The executive thus became a creature of the
legislature and his main function was to do the bidding of that body. He was deliberately not provided
with the tools necessary to ensure a vigorous leadership role; and what powers he had were specifically
enumerated. When asked how much power had been given

to the Governor of North Carolina under the new constitution, William Hooper of that state, answered: "Just enough to sign the receipt for his salary."[23] As Madison said "the legislature [was] omnipotent."[24]

The omnipotence of the legislatures is best seen in matters pertaining to legislation. This was the area of greatest frustration for the state governors. Except for New York and Massachusetts, which provided the executive with a veto power, there was no check on the legislature except by the other legislative house. In those states with a unicameral legislature, of course, even this check was not available. This led to legislative abuses. The number of bills passed during one session of the legislature and then promptly repealed during the next session is the best evidence of irresponsibility in that branch. Madison was disgusted with the "luxuriancy of legislation" which in the course of a few years

> . . . has filled as many pages as the century which preceded it . . . We daily see laws repealed or superseded before any trial can have been made [of] their merits, and even before a knowledge of them can have reached the remoter districts within which they are to operate.[25]

Richard Spaight of North Carolina complained:

> Our Constitution, unfortunately, has not been proved a sufficient check to prevent the intemperate and unjust proceedings of our legislature, though such a check would be very beneficial, and I think absolutely necessary for our well being."[26]

James Iredell, the crotchety political leader of North Carolina, a judge of that state and later its attorney general, vented his spleen thusly:

> The North Carolina laws of 1780 were the
> vilest collection of trash ever formed
> by a legislative body.[27]

This, in fact, was the general perception among political leaders in each of the states. The state constitutions generally did not provide the executive with the necessary power to prevent this abuse. James Madison concluded that "The executives of the States are in general little more than Cyphers."[28] This certainly would appear to be the case insofar as the constitutional powers of the executive, and the prestige of the executive under the state constitutions is concerned. It is remarkable that the executives were able to intervene as much as they did, given the polity of the period.

The exception to this general repression of executive power was New York where the state constitutional convention of 1777 created the strongest executive of any state. The debates pertaining to the executive actually included a suggestion that the executive should be given an absolute veto, thus making him "virtually a third house of the legislature."[29] This was, however, rejected and instead the veto power was placed in the hands of a Council of Revision consisting of the Governor, the Chancellor, and the judges of the Supreme Court. Although not as strong as an absolute veto would be, the Council of Revision was effective in curbing legislative abuse in New York. Governor Clinton and the Council of Revision vetoed 61 bills during the period under study. This was of paramount importance in advancing the cause of the strong executive with sufficient power to combat the legislature.[30] The New York executive was elected by the people to a three-year term with no limitation on reelection. Unlike other states, he thus was not dependent on the legislature for his appointment or continuance in office.

The State Executives

Most significant is the fact that election by the people was seen as an important change in the source of power. Under colonial rule the source of power was the King (acting through a surrogate governor); and in the other state constitutions, the legislature. In New York the source of power was the people. The Governor and the legislature depended on the people for their election and reelection.[31] Furthermore the Governor wielded the supreme executive power, and was commander in chief of state forces; he had the power to convene and prorogue the legislature; to grant reprieves and pardons, and recommend legislation. He was abjured to inform the legislature of the condition of the state, and "take care that the laws be faithfully executed." Of great importance is the fact that, unlike other state executives, the New York governor was not hampered in the day-to-day business of government by a Privy Council, which Jefferson, among others, considered to be a "fifth wheel."[32]

The New York governorship represented an important move in the direction of executive responsibility and independence, and away from the distrust and fear of a strong executive, which had earlier prevailed and which was manifested in the constitutions of the other states. James Wilson and Gouverneur Morris, who were probably more instrumental than anyone else at the Constitutional Convention in providing for a strong Presidency, looked to the New York executive as the model for the American president.

Many of the powers vested in the New York executive became subjects of debate in the Federal Convention, and were adopted by that body and incorporated into the Constitution of the United States. Resolution No. 8 of the Virginia Plan which was submitted to the Convention provided for a revisionary council similar in many respects to the Council of Revision in New York, even to the extent of including the national judiciary on that council.[33] Much of Article II, Section 3 of the Federal Constitution was derived from

the New York Constitution, most especially the felici-
tous expression which has provided the President with
much of his inherent powers: "He shall take Care that
the Laws be faithfully executed." The office of Vice
President and his duty as President of the Senate are
also found in the New York Constitution, which provided for a Lieutenant Governor who would serve as
President of the New York Senate. Finally, the requirement in the New York Constitution, that appointments be made "with the advice and consent" of the
Council of Appointment, can be considered the genesis
of the involvement of the Senate in the appointing
process at the federal level. The New York governor
was also largely the model used in establishing the
strong governor of Massachusetts.

Massachusetts was the last state to frame a new
constitution and benefitted from the experience of the
other states. The Massachusetts constitution was
adopted in 1780 although attempts had been made to
form a new government on several occasions after 1776,
especially in 1778 when a constitution was submitted
to the Massachusetts towns for their approval. Although this constitution was turned down, it is important in this study because of the extent of the evolutionary development of the executive and the new ideas
put forth under the Essex Result. In voting against
the proposed constitution, twelve towns in Essex
County, submitted a remarkably enlightened document,
known as the Essex Result, which included suggestions
for a better constitution. That part of the Result
pertaining to the executive is of particular interest.

In a nation and a state where fear of executive
power appears to have been dominant in the thinking of
Americans of the period, the Result advocated strength
in that office and authority sufficient to enable the
executive to defend himself from the encroachments of
the legislature; to maintain his independence, while
at the same time effectively performing the functions
of execution.

The Result also stressed separation of powers and a balanced system of government. It advocated that the three powers of government:

> be in different hands, and independent of one another, and so balanced, and each having that check upon the other, that their independence shall be preserved.

> If the three powers are united, the government will be absolute, <u>whether these powers are in the hands of one or a large number</u>.[34] [Emphasis in original]

The Result further suggested that the executive be a single person, elected annually at county conventions by electors previously chosen by the people. The electors would be equal to the number of representatives to which a county was entitled in the General Court.[35] This provision anticipated the Electoral College of the Federal system. In order to prevent any perpetuation of power in the hands of any one individual, Essex would limit incumbency to no more than three years in any six.[36]

The governor was to be given a veto power over the legislature to "prevent the latter from encroaching" on the executive:

> The executive power will be preserved entire -- the encroachments of the legislative will be repelled, and the powers of both be properly balanced.[37]

The Result argued that the governor would not make "an improper use of his negative" because he was elected annually and must account to the people each year.[38]

To those who were fearful of the veto power because of the colonial experience, the Result had this reassurance:

> This Governor is not appointed by a King, or his ministry, nor does he receive instructions from a party of men, who are pursuing an interest diametrically opposite to the good of the state. His interest is the same with that of every man in the state; and he knows he must soon return, and sink to a level with the rest of the community.[39]

When the Massachusetts constitutional convention met in 1779, it appointed a committee of thirty-one to draft a new constitution. That committee, in turn, named a subcommittee of three to prepare the draft. John Adams, James Bowdoin, and Samuel Adams comprised the subcommittee, but the actual author of the Massachusetts Constitution of 1780 was John Adams.[40] Adams was finally able to put into practice what he had been advocating for years as the type of government the states should adopt. He was also influenced by the experience of the other states as well as the reactions of the towns of Massachusetts to the 1778 constitution. Adams' idea of a suitable government was not a radical departure from colonial government. In fact, Adams wanted "to preserve the English Constitution in its spirit and substance, as far as the circumstances of this country required or would admit." He favored a government "as nearly resembling the Government under which we were born and lived." He thought it important to preserve the three branches of the legislature, which would include "an executive, independent of the senate or council, and the house."[41] Adams advocated a balanced system of government where no man or group of men would be allowed to dominate. This required that each department be independent of the others and able to check the others: "It is by balancing each of these powers against the other two, that the efforts in human nature towards tyranny can alone be checked."[42] He favored the doctrine of separation of powers as did the majority of delegates to the convention, but he realized that in order to provide the necessary checks each department must involve itself in the functions of the others. "Power must be opposed to power, force to force, strength to strength, interest to interest."[43]

Adams and many of his colleagues were impatient with legislative inefficiency and fearful of an unrestrained legislature. He rightly saw, as few people at the time did, that the real check on the legislature was a strong executive involved in legislative matters as an integral part of the legislature, "a third house". Thus, his draft of the 1780 constitution provided that the governor be given an absolute veto, and that a bill could not become a law without his signature. Adams considered the absolute veto power as especially necessary. He reasoned that "the executive power being an object of jealousy and envy to the people, and the legislature an object of their confidence and affection, the latter will always be able to render the former unpopular and undermine its influence" and for this reason an absolute veto was necessary to protect and strengthen the executive.[44] Furthermore, he could call the legislature into special session, and could prorogue it for a 90-day period in the event of disagreement on the date of adjournment. The executive was to be the main cog if this were to be an effective system of government. To strengthen further his hand in this respect he would be elected by the people and, in effect, become the only representative of all the people. In addition, although the governor would be elected annually, no limitation was placed on the number of consecutive terms he might serve. But, since executive actions also needed to be checked, Adams provided for a council of Senators selected by both houses to advise the governor. This would provide the necessary legislative oversight of the executive.[45]

The Convention, as one might expect, did not adopt the whole of Adams' proposal. The main objection was to the veto power, which the delegates considered to be too strong. A compromise was worked out granting the governor a qualified veto in which the veto could be overridden by a two-thirds vote of both houses.

The leaders of the convention recognized that the veto power would be one of the most controversial sections of the Massachusetts constitution. In the Address of the Convention, signed by James Bowdoin as President and submitted to the towns, the veto power was mentioned prominently and depicted in such a way as to persuade the towns of its necessity by stressing that the governor was the sole representative of all the people:

> The Power of Revising, and stating objections to any Bill or Resolve that shall be passed by the two Houses, we are of opinion ought to be lodged in the hands of some one person; not only to preserve the Laws from being unsystematical and inaccurate, but that a due balance may be preserved in the three capital powers of Government . . . The Governor is emphatically the Representative of the whole People at large. We have therefore thought it safest to rest this Power in his hands.[46] [Emphasis in original].

But in an effort to reassure the people concerning the exercise of this vast power by a single individual the Address also stated:

> To prevent the governor from abusing the Power which is necessary to put into his hands, we have provided that he shall have a Council to advise him at all

The State Executives

Times and upon all important Occasions.[47]

It should be noted that Chapter I, Article II of the Massachusetts Constitution, which covers the veto, is essentially the same as the veto provision in Article I, Section 7 of the Federal Constitution. The Framers of the Constitution thought the veto power exercised by one man, as in the Massachusetts constitution, far more effective than through a New York type Council of Revision.

Much of the reason for the more enlightened provisions of the New York and Massachusetts constitutions was the political involvement of the executive. Despite the constitutional limitations in the early state governments the executive office became a political one sought by the leaders of political factions within each state. The political development of the office was accelerated by the long and generally successful tenure of the state governors. Although ten states (New York, Delaware, and South Carolina were the exceptions) provided for a one year gubernatorial term, in practice governors in most states served for longer periods of time, being elected and reelected by either the legislatures or by the people. During the twelve-year period under study, both New Jersey and New York had only one Governor throughout the period. Only two men served as Governor in Massachusetts; three in Rhode Island, Connecticut, and New Hampshire; and four in Maryland.

Obviously those long tenures worked to the advantage of the executive, especially since the Whig philosophy that "when annual elections end there slavery begins,"[48] was also applied to the legislatures. Consequently, the lower houses of the legislature were also elected for one-year terms (except in South Carolina, which provided a two-year term). This affected the quality of representation in the legislature. The constant change in the legislature coupled with the continued reelection of the executive resulted in the executive having greater experience in government under the constitution than his legislative counterparts enjoyed, and also ensured an important continuity in the executive branch. This was a definite advantage which experienced politicians who became governors were bound to exploit.

The governors in this period were among the most popular, most experienced, and most prestigious men in their states. They led political factions by force of personality and exercised their power on the legislature through members of their personal party. That they were elected by overwhelming majorities, whether of the people or of the people's representatives, demonstrated great political strength. This is particularly evident in the administrations of George Clinton of New York; John Hancock and James Bowdoin in Massachusetts; Mesech Weare, John Langdon, and John Sullivan of New Hampshire; John Rutledge of South Carolina; Patrick Henry, Thomas Nelson, and Benjamin Harrison of Virginia; William Livingston of New Jersey; Caesar Rodney, John Dickinson, Thomas McKean, and George Read of Delaware; Benjamin Franklin, John Dickinson, and Joseph Reed in Pennsylvania; Thomas Johnson, Thomas Sim Lee, and William Paca of Maryland; Richard Caswell, Alexander Martin, and Samuel Johnston of North Carolina; William Greene, Jr., and John Collins of Rhode Island; and in Connecticut Jonathan Trumbull, (who had been colonial governor of that state and continued under the new government until 1784), Matthew Griswold, and Samuel Huntington.

These executives were not at all the "cyphers" that Madison described, despite the fact that they occupied offices made weak with limitations imposed by constitution. Constitutional provisions to the contrary notwithstanding, by dint of their own personality, popularity, and the exigencies of the day, the state executives of the period maintained a considerable amount of authority over their governments. They were able to a great extent to withstand legislative usurpation, to check unbridled legislatures, and to emerge as the most important and prestigious individuals in government. They were, in fact, the dominant leaders of their states during the entire period. To list the governors who served during the period from 1776 to 1788 is to list the principal political leaders of their states for the entire period. These governors were men of recognized ability.[49]

Only in Georgia can we find an exception. There, no one person, according to the state constitution could serve more than one year in three as governor. The result was that there were fifteen governors in twelve years. Obviously, none of these governors had the impact on their state that is evident in the other states.

The continued reelection of state governors and the increased prestige of the position -- a consequence of their successful tenures -- coupled with an increasing antipathy toward the legislative bodies, greatly reduced the earlier fears of executive power. The climate of public opinion changed between 1776 and 1787, most of all because the state executives did not attempt to control all of the functions of government or to act arbitrarily. Instead they attempted to provide a check against the strong legislatures. This check was not a constitutional one by means of the veto (except in New York and Massachusetts). Nevertheless, it was effective because of the energy and adroitness of the incumbent executive and the prestige and popularity which he had achieved.

In fact, among the great contributions of the state experience was the awakening to the need for a balanced system of government. This balance in government was brought about by a separation of functions and the establishment of coordinate responsibilities,[50] and is manifest in the New York and Massachusetts constitutions, which were among the last adopted. The New York and Massachusetts executives were best able to provide the necessary checks because of the manner of their election and the fact that a revisionary power was placed in their hands. In addition, although only the New York and North Carolina constitutions provided for the Governor to recommend legislation, most governors continued the colonial practice of addressing the legislature at the commencement of their session, and this led to initiation of legislation by the governor. Thus, the governors became involved in the legislative function with an important contribution toward the adoption of legislation. How he would implement his recommendations and how he would influence the passage of legislation would depend on the individual chief executive, his character, style, and personality. It is obvious, however, that much of the important statewide (as opposed to local interest) legislation passed by the states during the period was initiated by the governors, sometimes with the help of their Councils. The state governor, therefore, contrary to generally accepted views, did involve himself in the legislative function and provided a check of sorts to precipitate legislation. His successful actions in this regard contributed to the system of checks and balances which characterize the Federal constitution.

In the important area of policy-making, it is evident that these experienced governors had an impact. Strong governors, with long tenures in office, were able to dominate their councils and to become the interpretors of policy. In Pennsylvania the constitutional requirement that the Executive Council "prepare such business as may appear to them necessary to lay before the General Assembly," permitted such strong Presidents as Joseph Reed, John Dickinson, and Benjamin Franklin to influence policy.[51] Dickinson successfully lobbied to secure Pennsylvania's support to grant Congress the power to control commerce.[52] Franklin succeeded in having the very controversial test laws of Pennsylvania repealed.[53] There are many instances of Reed's intervention in policy-making. Among these was his insistence that Pennsylvania declare martial law when the British invaded the state.[54] In Maryland Governor Thomas Johnson was most influential in postponing ratification of the Articles of Confederation until all states agreed to surrender western land claims.[55] Maryland's support of the impost proposed by Congress was due to the work of Governor William Paca.[56] William Livingston, Governor of New Jersey, was a leader in the move to grant Congress powers to regulate trade.[57] The governors in all of the states exerted an important influence on state policy.

The effectiveness of the governors was also strengthened by the fact that the legislatures sat briefly and at great intervals. During the Revolution, particularly, when enemy activity caused legislatures to meet briefly and sporadically, the governor became the focal point of power. Indeed, much of the development of executive strength, responsibility, and authority can be traced to the Revolutionary era. According to one authority "the war was most instrumental in the change of attitude of the governor and the legislature toward each other,"[58] and contributed as well to the change of perception of executive power among the people. Because the legislature could not meet continuously, the governor had to act as the representative of the state in all matters, particularly those pertaining to the war. This was especially true in the South where the exigencies of war prevented the legislature from meeting. In several cases the legislature saw fit to provide the executive with temporary emergency powers which he could wield as a virtual dictator. On February 22, 1777 the Georgia legislature called on the President "to take upon himself the whole executive powers of government." A year later the Georgia Council instructed the Governor to act "as to him shall seem most eligible without advising with them unless when and where he shall find it convenient."[59] In 1778, and again in

1780, the South Carolina legislature granted Governor
Rutledge the power "to do everything necessary for the
public good except the taking away of the life of a
citizen without a legal trial."[60] In 1777 and 1778
Governor William Livingston of New Jersey, persuaded
the assembly to place him at the head of a special
Council of Safety which became the de facto government
of the state.[61] The prestige of the governors was
enhanced by their role as commander in chief of state
forces and their involvement in the war effort. Governors were in close communication with General Washington, and other commanders of the Continental Army. The
British on several occasions attempted to capture the
governor and thus complete the conquest of the state.
During wartime the legislature and the people looked
to the governor for leadership.[62]

The outstanding performance of state governors
during the war and their willingness to relinquish the
emergency powers granted to them definitely contributed to the change in political thought respecting the
executive. The commander in chief clause in the
federal constitution reflects the appreciation by the
Framers of the need for a central authority in time of
war or internal crisis. The manner in which the state
governors discharged this responsibility was evidence
that such a power could be safely lodged in the executive.

Congress, also, looked to the governors as the
heads of state, and communicated directly with them
respecting decisons made by Congress, as well as to
enlist their support for measures affecting the
states. In this respect, it is fortunate that many of
the governors had also served in Congress and consequently knew the workings of that body as well as the
difficulties faced by the Confederation. Congress, on
many occasions, empowered the governors to perform
investigations and discharge other duties for the
central government.

The State Executives

Thus, the development of executive power in America was an evolutionary process which was hastened by the participation at the state level of important individuals who contributed immeasurably to the success of their states during the period. As Jackson Turner Main says: "The most significant development in the executive branch is the emergence of popular governors with popular support which strengthened their offices." These men "all forecast the emergence of the strong executive in America."[63]

The Presidency of the United States was a prime beneficiary of the change in political thought which occurred during the formative period of the nation at the state level, and the most important contributing factor in that change was the effectiveness of the state chief executives. The constitutional and political development of the executive office at the state level impressed the Framers of the Constitution with the necessity of a strong executive.

Charles Thach, an authority on the creation of the American Presidency, credits state experience as the progenitor of the Presidency. He concludes:

> State experience had a definite, positive value. It taught that executive energy and responsibility are inversely proportional to executive size; that, consequently, the one-man executive is best. It taught the value of integration; the necessity of executive appointments, civil and military; the futility of legislative military control. It demonstrated the necessity for the veto as a protective measure. It showed that this power could be utilized as a means of preventing unwise legislation. It even . . . revealed the desirability of bringing legislative business into a single whole by the executive

department. It demonstrated the value
of a fixed executive salary which the
legislature could not reduce. It dis-
credited choice by the legislature....[64]

CHAPTER TWO

The Confederation Executive

The First Continental Congress which met on September 5, 1774 was never intended to evolve into the government of a nation or even the supreme legislative body of a nation. The Congress was just what the definition states, a meeting of constituent organizations interested in, and seeking a solution to a common problem, to wit: the change in attitude of England towards the American colonies. It was not the first time a Congress had assembled in America -- the Albany Congress had met in 1754, and the Stamp Act Congress in 1765. The delegates were actually representing separate and distinct colonial governments which would not necessarily be bound by any decision made by the Congress. The Congress, therefore, had no authority to act except as the individual delegates were bound by their own colony's instructions. As John Rutledge of South Carolina said in Congress: "We have no legal authority . . . We have no coercive or legislative authority. Our constituents are bound only in honour, to observe our determinations."[1] Despite this general lack of authority, the Congress adopted a number of resolutions, including economic sanctions, before its adjournment on October 26th. Each of the colonies adhered to the Congress' decisions, just as if their own legislatures had acted.

The Second Continental Congress convened on May 10, 1775, and immediately faced the conflict between the British and Americans at Lexington and Concord and the siege of Boston by the militia of the New England states. Because of the growing tensions, the government of Massachusetts was in disarray; concern for the future was manifest in every colony. Although it still lacked any "coercive or legislative authority," the Congress declared that the militia around Boston now constituted the "Army of the United Colonies." It named George Washington commander of American forces, and then appointed other generals. All of these decisions were tacitly approved by each of the colonies even though, in effect, they represented a commitment to resist British actions. This surprising acceptance of Congress as the leader in dealing with England was undoubtedly due to the caliber of men selected as delegates to the Congress -- they were the outstanding leaders in their states. They realized that the British use of force in Massachusetts was undoubtedly a prelude to similar actions against all the colonies. Whatever the reason, Congress became the avowed leader of thirteen colonies united against England. This did not imply that the colonies were united in a desire for independence: the spring of 1775 was much too early for serious consideration of such a move. But by July 1776, when Congress did declare independence, it had suggested to the colonies that they renounce allegiance to the King and reform themselves as separate states. Again, the authority of Congress is apparent in the positive actions taken by the states to implement these suggestions. The authority of Congress was especially acknowledged during the Revolutionary War, but there was a marked deterioration in the support given to it by the states following the Revolution. In fact, one of the faults of the Confederation was its inability to enlist support from the states.

The study of executive power in the Continental Congress makes clear the same fear of the strong executive as we noted when the first state constitutions were framed. The assumptions of republican polity, with its suspicion of executive power, are apparent in the effort to establish a permanent government under the Articles of Confederation.

There was no attempt to create a separate executive or an executive department. In his first draft of the Articles of Confederation, John Dickinson included a Council of State, which could have acted as an executive council. He envisioned it as a permanent body functioning independently of the Congress, in effect the executive arm of Congress. The Council would have the power to act for the Congress while in recess, particularly in matters concerning the military. It also would have the authority to make contracts and to draw on the treasury. Furthermore, the Council could call Congress into special session. Apparently, by making the Council a permanent body within the Congress -- even while the Congress sat -- Dickinson envisioned that the Council would act as an executive branch of government. The Council would be an _executive_ council.[2]

The delegates, however, were so distrustful of the executive power itself that the Council of State was eliminated from the final draft. In its place a Committee of the States was established to act in the name of Congress during its recess, but it would have no authority to act while Congress was in session. There was no apparent intent to make the Committee of States a permanent executive council. On the contrary, it is evident by its action in eliminating the Council of State that Congress was shying away from such a concept. There is, therefore, no mention in the Articles of an executive or a procedure for forming executive departments. Article IX merely empowered Congress to appoint "committees and civil officers as may be necessary for managing the general affairs of the United States under their direction."[3] The Articles clearly intended that the executive function was to be controlled by Congress. Generally recognized executive powers were specifically included among the powers of Congress. Consequently, as was the case in the states, the powers of government were in the hands of the legislature.

The selection of Peyton Randolph of Virginia as Chairman of the First Continental Congress was not intended to be an executive appointment. (The title was subsequently changed to President of Congress).[4] The President of Congress was first and foremost a delegate of his state and was allowed to vote with his state delegation. He was not given a tie-breaking vote. He could, and many times did, serve on congressional committees. The Articles of Confederation did not change the status of the President. He was still essentially the presiding officer of the Congress, appointed for a one-year term and forbidden from serving "more than one year in any term of three years."[5] Yet, despite the obvious lack of executive power given to the President under the Articles, it was, from the very beginning, a much sought after position.[6] The fourteen men selected to this office (John Hancock and Peyton Randolph were twice elected during the period of the Continental Congress and the Confederation) were all well-known and highly respected individuals. Thus, at the outset, the Presidency became a prestigious position. The President was an important national figure, whom Alexander Hamilton contended outranked any state governor. However, although the President was a substantial figure, it is also a fact that the office was "more honorable than powerful."[7] Article IX merely stated that he was to be appointed "to preside." But, despite the apparent limitations, his main duty, in addition to presiding, became that of the administrative head of government. This consisted mainly of carrying on correspondence with state officials, military personnel, representatives abroad, and foreign diplomats. In addition, he was the official representative of the Congress in dealing with outside authorities. The President of Congress was required to do a considerable amount of entertaining. In recognition of this he was given an allowance for entertainment and was furnished with "a house, table, carriage and servants." The duties of President became quite onerous and most of those serving in that capacity would have agreed with John Hancock that "I am almost hurried out of my life."[8] An authority on the subject, Jennings Sanders, points out, however, that the administrative details connected with the office declined after the Revolution when much of the administrative work formerly done by the President was taken over by the heads of the newly established executive departments.[9]

Nevertheless, the President continued to act as chief of state, a function that was carried over to the Presidency at the Constitutional Convention. In fact a unique feature of the American Presidency is that the President is at one and the same time chief of state and head of government. The function of the President of the United States as chief of state can be traced to its roots in the office of President of Congress under the Articles, even as the title itself is found there, and despite the fact that the President of the United States has no presiding duties.[10]

The President of Congress was never the chief executive of the Confederation, but the fact that the President was called upon to perform duties normally reserved for an executive, led to his acceptance by the people and the state executives as the leader of Congress and the head of the Confederation. This would influence the delegates to the Constitutional Convention to consider providing for a one-man executive.[11]

Another important appointment contributing to the evolution of executive power was that of Charles Thomson as Secretary of Congress. Thomson was from Pennsylvania and not a delegate. Appointed on September 5, 1774, he continued to be reappointed each year until 1789, working closely with each of the Presidents of the Congress. Thus he provided the continuity so essential in a body whose personnel was continually changing. Because of his long tenure in office he was the _de facto_ leader of Congress. He even served as interim President in 1777, although still not a delegate. He was called upon on many occasions to substitute for the President. Many times he intervened in congressional debates. He acted as the administrative assistant to the President in areas that could be construed as executive in nature, and when departments of government were created, he became involved in the work of every department.[12] In 1785 the French consul reported to Paris that Thomson was "a man wise, uniform, and full of moderation. The confidence of Congress in him has no limits."[13] He was an adept politician, always influential, and undoubtedly the most knowledgeable individual on the imperfections of the Articles of Confederation and the weaknesses of Congress.

In 1774, when Congress still considered itself nothing more than a meeting of delegates attempting to resolve a problem, it appointed committees whose duties seemed to be no more than to draft responses dealing with the English crisis. They were, however, legitimate legislative committees which brought about the consensus that resulted in the strong actions taken by the First Continental Congress. However, in 1775, after establishing an army, appointing generals, and accepting the necessity of resistance, Congress became a council of war, creating committees to deal with specific problems of war. These were the first executive committees. This Second Continental Congress actually appointed 102 committees to deal with such matters as manufacturing saltpeter, establishing a spy system, producing salt, procuring beef, and obtaining clothing. There were also hospital and medical committees, a committee on health and discipline, and a committee to recruit and maintain the cavalry. There was a committee formed to fortify the Hudson River and one to devise a strategy for intercepting two British ships. Another committee was to study the feasibility of obtaining a swift ship to intercept enemy vessels carrying stores.[14] There was, in short, a proliferation of committees, all manned by delegates to the Congress. John Adams complained that he was a member of 80 to 90 committees and was also expected to attend the meetings of Congress. His work day often commenced at four o'clock in the morning and continued until ten o'clock in the evening.[15] Since the committees were given little clerical help, the committee chairmen did most of the work.[16]

These committees, although executive in nature, had little authority. They reported the results of their deliberations to Congress; Congress decided what was to be done, involving itself in the most minute details of the committees' plans. Obviously this led to inefficiency and a waste of time and effort. On many occasions a committee reported to Congress, which after debating the report, appointed another committee to implement its policy. Thus, on receiving a report on October 5, 1775, that "two vessels loaded with powder and munitions had sailed from England for Quebec," Congress appointed a committee "to prepare a plan for intercepting" the vessels. When the committee reported on the plan that it had concocted, Congress appointed another committee to carry out the plan.[17]

These special committees were soon superseded by standing committees with more general authority. A Committee of Commerce was appointed in September 1775 and a Committee of Correspondence in November. The committee to intercept the two British ships was enlarged on October 30, 1775, and became the Naval Committee. Other standing committees were appointed which assumed the functions of the special committees. This tended to reduce the number of special committees, but it did not result in any great improvement in the efficiency of congressional operations. The standing committees still reported to Congress, which still debated their reports, and Congress still made the decisions about implementation. Periodically, the membership of standing committees changed because of the fluctuation in the state delegations in Congress. In many cases no permanent chairman was named making it difficult to fix responsibility.[18] Furthermore, there was considerable friction among committee members. In September 1775, John Adams commented in his Diary:

> It is almost impossible to move any Thing but you instantly see private Friendships and Enmities, and provincial Views and Prejudices, intermingle in the Consultation. These are degrees of Corruption. They are Deviations from the public Interest, and from Rectitude.[19]

Such jealousies, prejudices, parochialism, as well as the fear of monarchy, continued to plague Congress and the Confederation throughout their existence. In 1783 Samuel Osgood stated that the "great officers of state," that is the chairmen of congressional committees, were a step toward monarchy.[20]

These attitudes contributed to the inefficiency of the Congress in its attempt to discharge its executive function, and hampered the Congress in performing its important legislative duties as well. As Alexander Hamilton would remark: "Congress is properly a deliberative corps. It forgets itself when it attempts to play the executive."[21]

Although this inefficiency would continue throughout the Confederation period, there were some procedural improvements made which did help matters. One of these was the establishment on June 12, 1776, of the Board of War and Ordnance, directly attributable to General Washington's insistence that the war effort was being imperiled by the inefficiency of congressional committees.[22] This began the transformation of standing committees into boards, some of whose members were not delegates to Congress. Since these "outsiders" were a more permanent group, not subject to electoral shifts, they ran the boards and performed the administrative functions as well. This impressed Robert Morris with the necessity of establishing permanent executive offices. On December 16, 1776 he suggested in a letter to the Committee of Secret Correspondence, that Congress

> pay good executive men to do their business as it ought to be done. No man living can attend the daily deliberations of Congress and do executive parts of business at the same time.[23]

As a consequence of such pressures to improve the executive function, more changes were made in the structure of the executive boards. In the case of the Board of War, the volume of work mandated an even more permanent board. Thus, on October 17, 1777 a new Board of War, consisting of five nonmembers of Congress, came into being, although it was supervised by the old Board of War, which was its spokesman in Congress.[24] Since the newly created boards still reported to Congress, their reports were still subject to congressional change.

A continuing criticism of the board system was the absence of a single responsible individual at the head, and the difficulty of assessing blame and responsibility. The result was a failure of coordination between Congress and the boards. Nevertheless, the formation of boards was a step in the right direction and contributed to the establishment on January 10, 1781 of a Secretary for Foreign Affairs as the first executive department of the Confederation. This initial step was quickly followed on February 6 by the formation of the separate Departments of War, Marine, and Treasury.[25]

The movement towards the creation of executive departments was inexorable: the entire Congress, obviously, could not handle the myriad details of governing. Yet, there were some among the delegates who still objected to the establishment of departments because executive power and prerogatives would be placed in the hands of individuals.[26] General Washington, however, was insistent that the move would achieve greater efficiency: "Men of abilities at the head of the respective departments will soon introduce system, order, and economy." John Adams also supported the change.[27] Hamilton, of course, was the great advocate of executive departments under single heads because "there is always more decision, more despatch, more secrecy, more responsibility where single men than where bodies are concerned."[28] Louis Otto, the French representative, who pushed the reform from behind the scenes, wrote to the Comte de Vergennes:

> The various departments have been arranged in the most perfect manner; a regular system has been introduced into all the branches of the general administration.[29]

We must note, however, that, in establishing departments, Congress did not completely surrender its executive power and "its right to interfere in the basic operations of the departments."[30] A study of the individual departments shows this to be the case, although the new department heads, while working under difficult conditions, did bring some order out of chaos.

Department Of The Treasury

By far the most important matter facing Congress in 1781, and which plagued its deliberations throughout the period of the Confederacy, was finance. When the Treasury Department was established, Congress called Robert Morris to be Superintendent of Finance. Morris was an excellent choice. He had been a delegate to Congress, and an outspoken opponent of the committee system. He had demonstrated his leadership when Congress fled Philadelphia for Baltimore in December, 1776, remaining in Philadelphia as chairman of the committee representing the interests of Congress with "powers to execute such continental business as may be proper and necessary. . . ." In 1778 he chaired the standing committee of finance, where he demonstrated his capacity to handle such responsibilities.[31] He was well known in American financial circles and was probably the most qualified person available for the position. Morris, now out of Congress, was reluctant to accept the post of Superintendent of Finance and would not agree to take the office until he had wrung important concessions from Congress enabling him to function independently. Congress agreed to grant him all the latitude he needed to control his department and his subordinates: it reserved only the right of appointment.[32] Morris assumed his office on May 14, 1781, and three days later proposed to Congress that a national bank be established. On May 26 Congress agreed, but it was not until January 7, 1782 that the Bank of North America commenced operations. Morris had insisted, and Congress suggested to the states, that no similar bank be allowed to operate during the war. Congress also agreed with Morris that the bank's notes should be acceptable in payment of all taxes, duties, and debts of the United States.[33] There were many in Congress, however, who opposed the establishment of the bank and particularly opposed Morris' appointment. Continued attacks would be made on both, but Morris' competency was clearly evident. The bank's notes quickly provided a stable medium of exchange. On July 29, 1781, the Connecticut delegation reported to their governor that "The Financers notes and bank bills are in full credit and paid on sight, and are preferred to money . . . ."[34]

The value of a department headed by a single, responsible individual was shown when Morris proposed to Congress that the method of procuring supplies for the army be put on a contractual basis under the Treasury Department, and subject to bidding. His purpose was to eliminate corruption, delay, and extravagance.[35] Congress accepted Morris' proposals, which General Washington heartily approved; he had complained that "our posts cannot be maintained, nor the army be kept in the field much longer," if the system of procurement was not improved. Morris and his department were in a far better position to supervise the purchase and delivery of supplies than the congressional committees and boards had been able to do.[36]

Morris' main endeavor in 1781 was to maintain a regular and adequate supply for the army. To accomplish this, he continually applied pressure on Congress to grant him greater authority over procurement and distribution. Congress cooperated despite the misgivings of some delegates who did not trust Morris. Morris was thus able to relieve Congress from involvement in details which could be handled more effectively by the Treasury Department. Joseph Reed, in November, 1781 stressed that Congress was "relieved from all business of deliberation or executive difficulty with which money is in any respect connected. . . ."[37]

Although Morris was able to make inroads in resolving the financial difficulties of the Confederation through the use of Bank of North America notes, as well as his own "Morris Notes," he had to deal with the continuing problem of inflation and the states' failure to cooperate by providing the funds necessary to support the war effort and to pay interest on the debt. Congress had introduced a system of requisitions on the states but not all of the states met their quota. In 1781 Congress had proposed a duty on imported commodities to meet the financial needs of the Confederation. This impost, as it was known, was rejected because all states would not agree to it. Shortly after Yorktown, in 1782, Morris reported to Congress that since the impost had not been accepted by the states, the Confederation could not pay even the interest on its debt. This contributed to drying up any other source of income, domestic or foreign.[38]

Morris submitted a comprehensive, wide-ranging plan to resolve the financial difficulties of the Confederation and to restore public credit. It required use of the impost which had not been approved by the states, as well as taxes on lands ceded to the Confederation by the states. Congress rejected his plan as politically impossible.[39]

Morris was the leading policymaker of the 1780's.[40] Many in Congress were relieved to have a knowledgeable individual at the head of this important department and, because of his expertise, were inclined to support his program. Madison, in particular, was quite supportive. On June 4, 1782, he informed Edmund Pendleton: "Every member in Congress must be sensible of the benefit which has accrued to the public from his administration." Morris was even called upon to act as the temporary Secretary for Foreign Affairs in order to receive the first Dutch minister to the United States.[41] But throughout his term in office Morris was under attack by those who did not trust him personally or who opposed establishing the kind of power base he thought was necessary.[42] Arthur Lee feared that the result would be an oligarchy headed by Morris.[43] In 1783 Samuel Osgood led a movement in Congress to remove him. Osgood resented Morris' success in extracting concessions from Congress. He had been against the executive departments contending that they had been established with the connivance of France. He and others feared that the "great officers of state" were but a step toward monarchy.[44] Stephen Higginson also could hardly wait for Morris' resignation or dismissal. When Robert Livingston resigned as Secretary for Foreign Affairs in June 1783, Higginson "wish[ed] for one other removal and then I think Congress would be free of dangerous influences." He referred, of course, to Robert Morris.[45] These attacks made it increasingly difficult for Morris to achieve his goals.

Finally, in January 1783, a frustrated Morris gave notice, that should Congress and the states not take measures to establish a system of revenue, he would resign his office. At the time Congress faced a threat of an army uprising and called upon Morris to delay his resignation and to attempt to raise money for three months' pay for the army. Morris undertook the task only after receiving promises of congressional cooperation. When signs of cooperation did not appear, in March 1784 he submitted his resignation.[46]

Congress agreed to continue the Department of the Treasury, but under the aegis of a board of three commissioners -- all nonmembers of Congress. The Treasury Board, as it was called, had the same power and authority granted to Morris but was no more successful in resolving the problem of securing state funding than Morris had been. Again, much of the problem was the inability of Congress to act with vigor, given the jealousies and parochialism that John Adams had noted in 1775. For example, in 1786 the Treasury Board submitted a strongly worded requisition to the states with the warning that were the necessary funds not provided "nothing . . . can rescue us from bankruptcy, or preserve the Union of the several States from dissolution." Despite the threat, Congress refused to submit it to the states.[47]

Although the Department of the Treasury both under Morris and the Treasury Board failed to resolve the financial dilemma of the Confederation, it did relieve Congress of many executive burdens. Morris was able to bring a semblance of order to government financial practice. Unfortunately, the same cannot be said of the Treasury Board which succeeded him as is attested by the chaotic condition of finances when the new government commenced operations in 1789.[48]

The Confederation Executive

Department for Foreign Affairs

The genesis of the Department for Foreign Affairs was the Committee of Correspondence which Congress appointed in November, 1775 "for the sole purpose of corresponding with our friends in Great Britain, Ireland, and other parts of the world." The avowed purpose was to gather intelligence for Congress, which gave the Committee sufficient authority to act and provided it with a modest amount of money to accomplish its ends. Congress, of course, reserved the right to examine the correspondence at any time.[49] The committee subsequently changed its name to the Committee of Secret Correspondence.

The committee was very energetic and effective. Initially, its main contacts abroad were American agents in England, especially Charles Lee, to whom it wrote: "It would be agreeable to Congress to know the disposition of foreign powers towards us."[50] This led to the arrangements with Pierre A. Caron de Beaumarchais to provide secret aid from France to the United States. Benjamin Franklin, was a member of the committee, and contacted his friend in Holland, Charles Dumas, who was placed on the payroll and who provided important information and assistance. Furthermore, committee members met with Achard de Bonvouloir, a secret observer, sent to the United States by the French government. Bonvouloir assured the committee of French sympathty for the American cause. On the basis of this assurance the committee sent Silas Deane to France to represent Congress, "there to transact such business, commercial and political, as we have committed to his care." It is interesting to note that Congress as a whole was not privy to any of these transactions. Complete secrecy was maintained within the committee.[51]

After its initial spurt of activity the committee was less effective. It became a standing committee in 1777 -- Committee for Foreign Affairs -- but

43

this did not revive it. Membership dwindled to one member, the hard-working James Lovell. He complained that he had no secretary or clerk and that the committee's records were not in his hands but in those of the Secretary of Congress and that "there is no such thing as a Committee of Foreign Affairs existing."[52] Lovell was a member of Congress and had other duties to perform, which meant that many requests from agents abroad went unanswered or were greatly delayed. John Jay complained in 1780 that "one good private correspondent would be worth twenty standing committees, made up of the wisest heads in America, for purposes of intelligence."[53]

The movement to revitalize the executive functions of Congress led to the establishment on January 6, 1781 of the Department for Foreign Affairs but, because of factional rivalries in Congress, it was not until August that Robert Livingston was finally appointed to head the department. John Adams was especially pleased, both by the establishment of the department and by the appointment of Livingston, since this would result in "order . . . constancy . . . and activity."[54]

Essentially, the duties of the Secretary for Foreign Affairs were to communicate with agents abroad and to deal with foreign ministers. He was authorized to attend meetings of Congress and was admonished to keep Congress informed of all matters pertaining to his department. Indeed, almost immediately after the appointment one could note a marked improvement in communications, with Livingston reporting to Congress on many occasions about the work of American agents abroad. Livingston's activities were somewhat suspect in some quarters, however, because of his close relationship with the French minister. Those members of Congress who feared that France wanted to direct American foreign policy inclined to the belief that Livingston might be no more than an instrument of French policy. As in the case of Robert Morris, there

were factions in Congress who were against Livingston
and opposed the creation of the department. These
pressures, plus the fact that he had been appointed
Chancellor of New York, led to Livingston's resignation and departure in June 1783.[55]

The controversy in Congress about excessive
French influence in the department and the search for
a replacement acceptable to a majority delayed the
appointment of a new secretary for a year. Meanwhile,
the President and the Secretary of Congress assumed
the duties of head of foreign affairs. Finally, when
it learned that he was free to return from Europe,
Congress appointed John Jay Secretary for Foreign
Affairs and he began his tenure early in 1785.

Jay's appointment was a popular one. Those who
had suspected that France had been instrumental in
setting up the new departments of government and who
worried about undue French influence on them were
satisfied that Jay would not succumb to French blan-
dishments because he had shown his mettle in the
diplomacy ending the Revolution. Jay was, moreover,
particularly well qualified for the position. He had
served in the First and Second Congress, had been a
member of the Committee of Secret Correspondence, and
an active participant in its work. He was elected
President of Congress in 1778. Appointed Minister
Plenipotentiary to Spain in 1780, he served for two
fruitless years trying to obtain financial aid for the
United States. Later he was appointed to the peace
commission. Jay, therefore, brought to the office
knowledge of the workings of Congress, as well as
practical experience in foreign affairs.

He demonstrated his capacity immediately upon
assuming office. Despite the restrictions imposed by
Congress on the office, Jay became Secretary for
Foreign Affairs in fact as well as in name. He insisted on his exclusive right to select and appoint his
clerks. Furthermore, he required that all correspond-

ence come directly to him, bypassing Congress. The Congress agreed to these stipulations, acknowledging his expertise by permitting him to direct American agents abroad in all affairs.

The question of foreign loans was Jay's major preoccupation, one he shared with the Secretary of the Treasury. There were four additional major diplomatic problems that demanded his attention:

(1) Commercial treaties: Jay enjoyed his greatest successes in this field. By the close of 1786 arrangements were concluded with the Netherlands, Sweden, and Prussia.[56]

(2) The frontier posts: an important problem affecting American security, which was not settled until 1794.

(3) American commercial penetration of the British and French empires: a consular agreement was reached with France, but England remained unmoveable until 1794.

(4) Navigation of the Mississippi River: a treaty was concluded during Jay's tenure but rejected by Congress. The question was not resolved until 1795.[57]

Jay's expertise in foreign affairs, as well as his long tenure, freed him from congressional interference, particularly during the last days of the Confederation when Congress grew even weaker, as Jay's influence became stronger. The French minister, reported to Paris that Jay "especially has acquired a peculiar ascendancy over the members of Congress. Congress seldom has an opinion different from his."[58] Indeed, Henry P. Learned contends that Jay was "the chief executive of the Confederation."[59]

His performance as Secretary for Foreign Affairs pointed up the importance of having single heads of

departments and also <u>executive</u> departments. This influenced delegates to the Constitutional Convention of
1787 that the new government must be similarly structured.

Department of War

The Department of War was established on February
7, 1781, but eight months of congressional wrangling
delayed Benjamin Lincoln's appointment as the first
Secretary of the department. Lincoln served during the
period of the army's disbandment. He resigned in
October 1783, when the department reverted to the
chief clerk until the appointment of Henry Knox as
Secretary in March 1785. Knox served until the end of
the Confederation period, and remained as Secretary of
War under the Constitution. His chief duties concerned the administration and protection of the Western Territories, the main emphasis of the Department
of War under the new government. Shays's Rebellion in
Massachusetts gave Congress occasion to send him to
that state to protect the arsenal at Springfield.
Upon his return he reported on the seriousness of the
incident and recommended increasing the size of the
continental army in order to quell this rebellion and
to meet future emergencies. Shays's Rebellion and
Knox's report brought home to congressional leaders
the inability of the Confederation to deal with such
emergencies. It persuaded many that the Articles must
be changed in favor of strengthening the central government.

. . . . .

In summary, the transformation of political
thought, which at the state level led toward the
creation of a strong executive, was apparent also at
the national level, even under the Articles of Confederation. The evolution of executive management can
be seen in the development of a system of administration, distinct from legislation: the administration of
policy, efficiently and effectively. The move away

from congressional committees to executive boards independent from Congress finally led to the establishment of departments headed by single executives. The quality of the appointed heads of department, their expertise, and their performance in office led to further relinquishment of executive powers by Congress. The change in the membership of Congress, as well as the diminished importance of the institution in the post-war years also contributed to greater reliance on the heads of departments. Continuity in government -- an attribute of the executive -- was achieved by the long tenure in office of the Secretary of Congress, Charles Thomson, and Secretaries Jay and Knox.[60] Jay, above all, became the executive in matters of foreign affairs; Congress deferred also to the Secretary of War, Henry Knox, on military questions involving the Western Territories, and Shays's Rebellion.

These changes in the executive structure of Congress were inspired not by theoretical studies but by practical necessities. It had become apparent that a legislative body was inadequate to the tasks of executive functions. The Framers of the Constitution, many of whom had served in the Continental Congress, recognized such inadequacies by agreeing -- without debate -- to the establishment of an executive branch of government.[61]

The Confederation experience also is evident in some of the provisions of Article II of the Constitution. The title of President can be traced to the Confederation, as well as the emergence of the President as Chief of State and Head of Government. The prestige of the office of President of Congress, and the high regard in which it was held, contributed to the type of executive office that was created. The executive departments established under the Constitution were, in effect, a continuation of the departments which functioned in the Confederation. The power granted to the President to make treaties was an outgrowth of a similar grant of power given by Congress to Secretary John Jay.

Although the experience of the executive at the state level was the most important contributing factor in the development of the Chief Executive of the United States, the experiences under the Confederation were also of great importance. These eventually led to the creation of the Presidency at the Constitutional Convention in 1787.

CREATING THE AMERICAN PRESIDENCY 1775-1789

PART II

The Constitutional Executive

CHAPTER THREE

The Executive in the Constitutional Convention

Establishing a separate executive department of government was not the main reason for calling the Constitutional Convention in 1787. However, the lack of a constitutional executive was one of the inadequacies of the Articles of Confederation that the Convention was called to correct in order to render "the federal constitution adequate to the exigencies of government and the preservation of the Union."[1]

There had been general dissatisfaction with the Articles among nationalists who wanted a stronger central government. The weakness of the Confederation in the post-war years, especially in matters of finance, was attributed to the provisions in the Articles requiring unanimous assent of the thirteen state legislatures before the Articles could be amended. The amendment of this provision and the introduction of other improvements had been discussed since 1780.

The move to amend the Articles of Confederation was spearheaded by Alexander Hamilton and James Madison at the Annapolis Convention in September 1786. This was a meeting of trade commissioners from five states seeking uniform commercial regulations. The Convention submitted a resolution to the states calling for a convention of all the states to meet the following May for the purpose of devising "such further provisions as shall appear to them necessary to render the constitution of the federal government adequate to the exigencies of the Union."[2] Seven state legislatures quickly agreed to attend such a convention. This appeal also coincided with Shays's Rebellion in Massachusetts, which further alarmed nationalists to the need for a strong government. This combination of events led Congress in February 1787 to call for the Convention to meet in Philadelphia in May 1787.[3]

Congress had set the date for the meeting of the Constitutional Convention as May 14, 1787, but on that date only the delegates from Pennsylvania and Virginia had arrived. Congress required that a majority of the states be present before the Convention began to conduct business. Therefore it was not until May 25 that the Convention first met.

There were seventy-four delegates elected by twelve states. Only Rhode Island refused the invitation. Fifty-five of these delegates attended the Convention. Max Farrand put the average attendance at forty or less.[4] No more than eleven states were represented at any time. New York sent three delegates, but two of them walked out, so that New York had no vote in the Convention after July 10. The New Hampshire delegation did not arrive until July 23.

Collectively the Framers were an impressive lot. Thomas Jefferson called them "an assembly of demigods,"[5] and Benjamin Franklin thought the Convention "the most august and respectable Assembly he ever was in in his life."[6]

Essentially, they were well educated, practical, experienced politicians. They were well suited for the task of constitution-making. Of the fifty-five men who attended the Convention, twenty-six were graduates from Princeton, Yale, Harvard, William and Mary, Columbia, the College of Philadelphia, Oxford, St.

Andrews, and the Middle Temple in London. In addition several had graduate degrees. There were thirty-three lawyers who had studied under men like Dickinson, Wythe, and Jefferson.[7] They were familiar with, and, when it would help their cause, could quote from, the works of Hobbes, Hume, Locke, Montesquieu, Blackstone, and from John Adams' recently published <u>Defence of the Constitutions of the United States</u>. Several, particularly Madison and Charles Pinckney, made a special effort before the convention to study the composition of governments in other parts of the world as well as the constitutions of the states.[8]

The Constitution has been called "a bundle of compromises" and certainly the big reason for this is that the Framers knew the importance of compromise and, therefore, of consensus. The common denominator among the delegates was the extensive practical political experience they had in federal and state politics. No less than thirty-eight of them had served in the Continental Congress. They knew the weaknesses of the Articles. They knew what changes were necessary to form an effective government. Forty-eight of the fifty-five delegates had served in state government. Eight of them had been governors or presidents of their states.

Furthermore, the Framers were not Johnny-come-latelys to the art of constitution-making. Sixteen had participated in constitutional conventions within their states and some had served on drafting committees of those conventions. Two of them, Dickinson and Sherman, had helped to draft the Articles of Confederation, and Charles Pinckney had chaired a committee of Congress to revise the Articles. The experience of the Framers is apparent in the fact that the Constitution is replete with clauses also found in the state constitutions or in the Articles of Confederation. The men who assembled at the State House in Philadelphia were well prepared, experienced in the art of government and constitution-making, and committed to the task of framing a national constitution. The Constitution was the product of this American experience derived at the state and federal level.

The first order of business on May 25, 1787, was the election of the President of the Convention. George Washington was unanimously elected. It was then determined that the proceedings of the convention would be conducted with the utmost secrecy. No verbatim notes were to be taken and the delegates were enjoined not to reveal any information about the proceedings "in order to secure unbiased discussion within doors, and to prevent misconceptions and misconstructions without".[9] In addition, according to a contemporary observer from Massachusetts who was visiting Philadelphia at the time, "Sentries are planted without and within . . . to prevent any person from approaching near . . . ."[10] Thomas Jefferson, among others, was critical of the secrecy imposed as "tying up the tongue of their members."[11] But Madison indicated many years later that without such a rule there would have been no Constitution.[12]

The main debates were conducted in the Committee of the Whole House, a device with which the delegates were familiar. Each morning after a short opening session the Convention would resolve itself into the Committee of the Whole to debate the structure of the Constitution. Nathaniel Gorham, of Massachusetts, who was at the time the President of Congress, was chosen Chairman of the Committee and he served in that capacity whenever it met. The Committee of the Whole met daily from May 30 until June 19 when it reported the result of its deliberations to the Convention. After that, all proceedings were conducted in Convention. Decisions in the Committee and in Convention were by majority vote of the states present.

The Convention sat from May 25 until September 17, meeting daily except Sundays, usually from 10 to 3 or 4, although on several occasions it sat for seven hours.[13] The Convention recessed for the Fourth of July, and adjourned from July 26 to August 6 while the Committee of Detail met.

At times the Convention referred those matters on which agreement could not be reached to special committees. The three most important committees insofar as the executive branch was concerned, were:

The Committee of Detail (also called the Committee of Five) which submitted the draft of a constitution.

The Committee on Remaining Matters, (Brearley Committee or Committee of Eleven) consisting of a member from each state, was appointed on August 31 and sat until September 5 when it submitted its last report.

The Committee on Style, appointed on September 8, reported the completed Constitution on September 12.

Three plans of government were formally submitted to the Convention and were considered by the Convention or by the committees: the Virginia Plan, Pinckney Plan, and New Jersey Plan. (The Hamilton Plan was put forward by Alexander Hamilton in his speech of June 18 but it was never presented for consideration). Many of the ideas and proposals incorporated in these plans eventually became part of the Constitution, but of them all the most important was the Virginia Plan, the first one submitted.

The Virginia Plan

The Virginia Plan was presented by Governor Edmund Randolph on May 29. It consisted of fifteen Resolutions which became the basis for discussion within the Committee of the Whole and, according to Madison, "the basis of its deliberations."[14] Historians generally agree that the plan was originally prepared by James Madison prior to the Convention and was discussed at caucuses of the Virginia delegation before a quorum arrived in Philadelphia. The seven-member Virginia delegation was the first in Philadelphia, the entire delegation having arrived by May 17. Madison himself never claimed exclusive credit for the plan, always attributing it to "the result of a consultation among the seven Virginia Deputies."[15]

The portion of the Virginia Plan concerning the executive appears as Resolutions 7 and 8:

Resolution 7 provided for a national executive but it did not indicate whether the executive would be composed of one or more persons. The executive would be appointed by the legislature, which was the usual form found in all state constitutions south of New York, and would be ineligible for reelection.[16] This was a departure from the state constitutions, all of which, except Delaware, permitted immediate reelection.

Under the plan, the executive was authorized to execute the national laws and was to "enjoy the Executive rights vested in Congress by the Confederation," although the Articles of Confederation did not specifically stipulate those rights. The powers of Congress under the Articles were all-encompassing: it performed all the functions of execution as well as those of legislation. Among the powers generally accepted as pertaining to the executive as enumerated in the Articles were the right to send and receive ambassadors, to enter into treaties and alliances, to appoint civil officers, to commission officers of the armed forces, and to direct the operations of the armed forces. Included among these powers was also "the sole and exclusive right and power of determining on peace and war." The last was objected to immediately at the Convention. General Charles Cotesworth Pinckney, of South Carolina, feared that "the executive powers of [the existing] Congress might extend to peace and war which would render the executive a monarchy of the worst kind, to wit an elective one."[17] All of the executive powers in the Articles would subsequently find their way into the Constitution as special powers granted either to the President or to Congress.

Resolution 8 of the Virginia Plan addressed the veto power. It provided that the executive and members of the judiciary would compose a Council of Revision with authority to veto legislative acts. This was similar to the New York Council of Revision.[18]

Although the Virginia Plan served a useful purpose in providing a basis for discussion, the only executive provisions of the plan retained in the Federal Constitution, in addition to instituting the office, were related to the execution of the laws and to executive compensation.[19] Far more influential in dealing with the executive was the Pinckney Plan.

The Pinckney Plan

The Pinckney Plan prepared by Charles Pinckney (cousin of General Pinckney mentioned previously) was presented on the same day as the Virginia Plan. This plan was referred to the Committee of the Whole but there was no discussion of it by that Committee or the Convention itself.[20] Referred to the Committee of Detail, however, this plan became the model on which the Constitution was based. It was a far more comprehensive plan of government than the Virginia Plan. The "committee took the Pinckney draught and worked on it from the preamble to the end, deleting, adding, and changing it."[21] Many of the provisions of the Constitution, particularly those that relate to the executive, are taken directly from the Pinckney Plan.

Charles Pinckney was a member of the Continental Congress from 1784 to 1786, where he noted the weaknesses of the Confederation and actively involved himself in attempts to improve the system. He advocated amendments to the Articles of Confederation that would "render the federal government adequate to the ends for which it was instituted." He addressed the New Jersey legislature in the same vein on March 13, 1786. On his appointment as a delegate to the Philadelphia Convention, Pinckney studied the various systems of government in the United States as well as earlier proposals for constitutional reform, culling from them those ideas that appealed to him.[22] The provisions of the Pinckney Plan relating to the executive were copied extensively from the constitutions of New York and Massachusetts.[23]

The plan provided that "the executive Authority of the U.S. shall be vested" in a single person with the title of President. He was to be chosen annually by joint ballot of the two houses of the legislature. The President was required to "attend to the execution of the laws," to inform the legislature periodically of the state of the union, and also to recommend measures for their consideration. He could convene the legislature in special session and could prorogue it when they could not agree on adjournment. The President was empowered to commission officers, as well as to suspend civil and military officers. He was authorized to communicate with the executives of the states. He was made commander in chief of the army, and admiral of the navy. He could seek advice from the "heads of the different departments as his Council."[24]

The veto power would be in the hands of a Council of Revision of which the President was a member. This was adapted from the New York constitution.[25]

Discussing Pinckney's contribution to the executive article in the Federal Constitution, Charles Thach says "his concept of what constituted executive power was remarkably complete, and his treatment of it far more satisfactory than that of the Virginia Plan," concluding that there "is sufficient warrant for attributing to Pinckney a very real influence on Article II of the finished Constitution."[26]

The Pinckney Plan had great impact on the Constitution and, we must presume, on the delegates. Yet, within the Convention, it was not subjected to debate as were the Virginia and New Jersey Plans.

The New Jersey Plan

On June 9 the New Jersey delegation reverted to the most controversial question before the Convention -- that of representation in the national legislature. This was a very divisive matter with the larger states desiring to dispense with the mode under the Articles of Confederation which provided for equal representation of the states in Congress, and to institute, instead, representation on the basis of population. David Brearley and William Paterson of New Jersey warned, that if representation were by population, their state would never agree to the Constitution. Paterson pointed out that the Convention had been called for the purpose of revising the Articles and not instituting an entirely new government. He agreed that the Articles must be revised, but he maintained that the federal system should be maintained: each state must be considered sovereign and equal to each of the others. Representation in the legislature should be equal, as among states. The larger states, of course, opposed this idea. The question was submitted to a vote and the Convention agreed to popular representation, but this did not end the controversy.[27] On June 15 Paterson presented a plan, prepared by members from Connecticut, New York, New Jersey, Delaware, and Maryland, known as the New Jersey Plan (or the Paterson Plan). It was, in fact, a plan of government based on the revision, correction, and enlargement of the Articles of Confederation. Article 4 dealt with the executive.[28]

This plan called for multiple executives, elected

by Congress, ineligible for a second term, and removable by Congress "on application by a majority" of the state executives. The executives under the plan would be the creatures of the legislature, under their domination, as well as dependent on the state governors for their continuance in office. The federal executives would execute federal laws, appoint federal officers, and direct military operations.[29]

The Committee of the Whole took up the plan on June 16. In discussion, the main point of contention was whether there should be a national government as had been accepted by the Committee of the Whole, or a federal government in all essentials like the Articles. The question of representation was a vital consideration. Debate continued until June 19, when the Committee voted against further consideration of the New Jersey Plan and agreed to report the amended Virginia Plan to the Convention.[30]

On June 20 the Convention opened debate on the proposals submitted by the Committee of the Whole. Resolutions 9 and 10 pertained to the executive. The Committee agreed that the executive would consist of a single person to be chosen by the national legislature for a single seven-year term. He was empowered to execute the national laws but was not given the power of appointment which was placed with the Senate. He could be impeached. He was granted the right to veto legislation, but this could be overridden by two-thirds of each branch of the legislature.[31]

The Convention debated these resolutions from June 20 until July 26, when they were submitted to the Committee of Detail.

The Committee of Detail

The Committee of Detail had five members, chosen, apparently, on the basis of geography. John Rutledge, the chairman, was from South Carolina, Edmund

The Executive in the Constitutional Convention

Randolph of Virginia, another southerner; Oliver Ellsworth of Connecticut and Nathaniel Gorham of Massachusetts represented the north; James Wilson was from the middle state of Pennsylvania. The committee was charged with "reporting a Constitution conformably to the Proceedings" of the Convention.[32] All resolutions adopted in Committee of the Whole and subsequently by the Convention, as well as the Virginia Plan, the Pinckney Plan, and the New Jersey Plan, were turned over to the Committee. No substantial change in the executive article reported by the Committee of the Whole had been made by the Convention.

The draft constitution prepared by the Committee of Detail was a remarkable document. Whereas the Convention preferred a general statement of executive power -- "power to carry into execution the national laws" -- the Committee saw fit to clothe him with broad, yet specific, powers which made the office formidable. The Committee also established the independence of the executive from the legislature by **vesting** the executive power in the President. The source of presidential power thus became the Constitution rather than the legislature. All of the powers provided in the Committee's draft found their way into the Constitution.[33]

The Committee's draft constitution was printed and submitted to the Convention on August 6.

Thus, the main elements of the Constitution were formulated. William R. Davie of North Carolina reported to James Iredell of the same state that "the great outlines are now marked, and have been detailed by a committee: the residue of the work will rather be tedious than difficult."[34]

The Convention's debates focused, of course, on the Committee's draft. On August 31 the Convention appointed a Committee on Remaining Matters and referred to it "the parts of the Constitution as have been postponed, and such parts of the report as have not been acted on"[35]

Committee on Remaining Matters

Where the Committee of Detail structured the executive article, it was left to the Committee on Remaining Matters to resolve the differences that remained.

The Committee consisted of a member from each state represented at the Convention. Among those Committee members considered as advocates of a strong executive were Gouverneur Morris, Rufus King, James Madison, John Dickinson, Daniel Carroll, and Pierce Butler.[36] This was a majority of the Committee. They could be expected to support any measure enhancing the powers of the President.

Those sections of the executive article referred to the Committee were: Impeachment, succession, treaty-making, and appointment of ambassadors and judges.

The Committee changed the impeachment provision by placing the trial of the President in the Senate instead of the Supreme Court, and it removed "corruption" as an impeachable offense.[37] The treaty-making power, which the Convention had lodged with the Senate, was given to the President who would act by and with the advice of two-thirds of the Senate. The President was also given the power of nominating and appointing ambassadors and judges, again with the advice and consent of the Senate.[38]

The most important contribution of the Committee was that it resolved the question of presidential selection, which James Wilson considered "the most difficult of all on which we have had to decide."[39] The Convention had since June 2 consistently favored legislative appointment. The delegates supporting a strong executive, however, argued that this would make the executive too dependent on the legislature and hence he could not provide the necessary check on that body. They proposed on seven different occasions that election be by the people or by electors. As matters stood on August 31 the Convention had agreed that the President was to be appointed by the legislature for a seven-year term and was ineligible for reelection. This was in keeping with the Virginia Plan.

Presidential tenure and reelection were tied to the question of selection. If the legislature was to appoint the President, then the consensus was that he should serve a longer term of six or seven years, without reelection. This, it was thought, would reduce his dependence on the legislature. Those favoring election by the people or by electors wanted a shorter term and eligibility for reelection.

These matters were not referred to the Committee on Remaining Matters but it would appear that Gouverneur Morris, who was a member of the Committee, took things into his own hands and proposed that these questions be considered. The result was that the Committee completely revamped the clause providing for election of the President by introducing the Electoral College system whereby the President would be elected by electors. This was obviously a compromise to secure nearly unanimous support within the Committee itself. Since the Committee was a microcosm of the Convention, approval by that body could also probably be obtained. The primary consideration was to enlist the backing of the smaller states which favored selection by the legislature as fairer to them than a popular election. It was, therefore, proposed that the electors be appointed by the states "in such manner as its legislature may direct." Obviously, the state legislature could opt for election directly by the people of the state or appointment by the state legislature. The importance of this provision was in placing the responsibility of selection of electors on the state legislature. To further emphasize the federal nature of the election process, the committee provided that the electors would cast their ballots within the states rather than at the seat of the national government. This would also meet any objections over the expense of transporting electors to such a central area, while removing the fears of cabal and corruption which could result if all electors met in one place at the same time. Furthermore, the plan required that each elector vote for two persons, "at least one of whom would not be an inhabitant of the state." This was designed to allay the fears of the smaller states that the President would always be from a large state. This provision also increased the possibility that no one candidate would receive a majority of the electoral votes, thus forcing a contingent election. The small states were further appeased by placing the contingent election in the hands of the Senate, where each state had an equal vote. Since it was generally conceded that "nineteen times in twenty" the election would be decided in the Senate, the approval of the small states to the plan was obtained.[40]

Having removed the President's dependence on the legislature for his election, the presidential term was now reduced from seven to four years, making the President more accountable. His eligibility for re-election was tacitly conceded. The Committee's plan also provided for a Vice-President. This solved the matter of presidential succession which had been referred to the Committee.[41]

The Committee also rejected the proposal that an Executive Council be established. It retained the clause authorizing the President to secure opinions in writing from the principal officers of the executive department.[42]

Finally, the Committee established the qualifications necessary to be President.[43]

The Executive in the Constitutional Convention

The Committee began reporting to the Convention the day after it was appointed and continued to do so until September 8. The Convention made some stylistic changes in the wording of the executive article and accepted the recommendations of the Committee.

The Committee of Style

The next step in the making of the constitution was to edit what had been done and "to revise the style of and arrange the articles which had been agreed to by the House."[44] A Committee of Style was therefore created consisting of William Johnson of Connecticut, Rufus King of Massachusetts, Alexander Hamilton, Gouverneur Morris, and Madison. It is generally agreed that Morris did most of the work in the Committee. In fact, many years later, in 1814, in a letter written to Timothy Pickering, Morris contended that "the instrument was written by the fingers which write this letter."[45]

Except for rearrangement of the clauses, slight modification of sentence structure, and removing redundancies, Morris and the Committee did not change the executive article. The Committee report was submitted to the Convention on September 12, where the only change to the executive article was to reduce the override of a veto from three-fourths to two-thirds of both houses of Congress.[46]

Its work done, the Convention voted to adopt the Constitution on September 15 and the Constitution was signed on September 17.

According to a recent study, twenty-one of the fifty-five members of the Convention played "important roles in the invention of the Presidency."[47] Of these twenty-one we can select six whose contributions were vital to the emergence of a strong executive. James Wilson, Gouverneur Morris, Elbridge Gerry, and Rufus King were adherents of a strong executive even before the Convention. Charles Pinckney's main contribution was the Pinckney Plan. James Madison is included in the group of six because he became convinced during the Convention of the need for a strong executive, having previously been uncertain and undecided as to just how the executive should be constituted.

Madison's uncertainty is evident in his letter to Washington dated April 16, 1787: "I have scarcely ventured as yet to form my own opinion, either of the manner in which [the executive] ought to be constituted or of the authorities with which it ought to be cloathed."[48] His early lack of commitment to an effective executive was voiced on June 1, during the first debate on a unitary executive, when he hedged his support by suggesting that before a decision could be made on the composition of the executive it was necessary "to fix the extent of the executive authority," to better determine "how far they might be safely entrusted to a single officer." Madison then introduced a motion empowering the executive to execute the national laws, and to appoint to offices in cases not otherwise provided for, as well as "other powers as may from time to time be delegated by the national Legislature."[49] Madison had not yet accepted the idea of "vesting" powers in the executive by constitutional mandate. Had Madison's ideas been followed, such important powers as those of the commander in chief, treaty making, and pardoning would have been subject to legislative control.

During the several debates on the executive he did support the advocates of a strong executive. His strong nationalist views, plus his understanding of the limitations of executive power at the state level, (especially in Virginia), together with the difficulties faced by the Confederation from the lack of an executive, led him to support measures that would ensure a strong independent executive. Madison's contributions to the executive, nevertheless, were more in support of the initiatives of others than of his

The Executive in the Constitutional Convention

own making.

The primary leader of those who advocated a strong executive at the Convention was James Wilson of Pennsylvania. Wilson had long been an advocate of executive strength and independence. He had led the fight against the Pennsylvania constitution, because among other things it lacked an effective executive, and his ideas on the executive were well developed by 1787. He admired the New York Constitution, which combined executive unity, a three-year tenure with no restriction on reelection, a vesting clause, specific enumerated powers, and a qualified veto. Wilson preferred, however, an absolute veto. He particularly liked the provision in the New York Constitution for popular elections. Wilson's commitment to strong executive power is apparent in the first debate on the subject in the Convention. He called for a single executive, elected by the people to a three-year term with the presumption of eligibility for reelection. Seeing that popular election would not be accepted, he introduced a motion on the following day proposing election by electors elected by the people. Despite the defeat of his motions, he reintroduced them on a number of occasions and supported all other motions designed to augment executive strength. In addition, he was the main advocate on the Committee of Detail of an independent and responsible executive and wrote into its report important provisions respecting the executive.

Charles Thach called Gouverneur Morris the "real floor leader" of the strong executive faction.[50] This would be especially true after July 2, when he returned to the Convention after a month's absence. Thereafter Morris was present every day and participated fully in the debates. His work on the Committee of Remaining Matters, and the Committee of Style, as well as on the floor of the Convention, place him, with Wilson, at the forefront in ensuring a strong Presidency.

The Constitutional Executive

Morris brought excellent credentials to the Convention. He had served on the committee to draft the New York Constitution and was mainly responsible for the executive structure of that plan. He had been interested in an absolute veto for the executive in New York, but, failing to achieve it, settled for the Council of Revision. In the 1787 Convention he spoke more than any other delegate. He supported Wilson in seeking a national government, including a strong executive, and the two men formed an effective team within the Pennsylvania delegation. Because of his absence, he did not participate in the preliminary debates in the Committee of the Whole, but it is evident that he supported Wilson's motions to ensure a strong executive. In discussing the report of the Committee of Detail on July 17, Morris found fault with legislative appointment of the executive because, together with the impeachment power, the executive would be rendered "the mere creature of the legislature." Morris insisted that the executive must be independent of the legislature, otherwise "usurpation and tyranny. . .will be the consequence."[51] When his motion to provide for direct election by the people was rejected by a 9 to 1 margin, Morris supported a motion to appoint the executive "during good behavior".[52]

In a long speech on July 19, Morris expounded his views on the executive, whom he saw as the linchpin of government and on whom "must depend the efficacy and ability of the Union". He espoused a doctrine of checks and balances permitting the executive to check legislative actions. He thought it an executive function and duty "to appoint the officers and to command the forces of the Republic," as well as all other officers including judges. He wanted the executive "so constituted as to be the great protector of the Mass of the people." If he was to be the "Guardian of the people" he should be elected by them. If he was to be a check on the legislature "let him not be impeachable." He preferred a short term with unlimited eligibility for reelection. On the other hand, if the legislature was to appoint the executive then he "saw no alternative for making the Executive independent of the legislature but . . . to give him his office for life".[53] Throughout the convention he pressed for a powerful executive, and the executive which emerged from the convention is in many respects the executive that Morris desired. There is little doubt about his influence on the Committee on Remaining Matters. He was the catalyst within that committee.

Elbridge Gerry of Massachusetts was also involved in every aspect of the debates on the Constitution. Accused of being a "Grumbeltonian" who objected "to everything he did not propose," and charged with inconsistency,[54] he was, nevertheless, very consistent in his insistence that the executive be strong enough to defend himself against the legislature. He supported a unitary executive, and strongly opposed election by the national legislature, to avoid which, he introduced several motions designed to interpose the states in the electoral process. He opposed restrictions on executive reelection, provided that the executive was independent; if, however, the legislature was to appoint the executive, then he preferred a long single term. Only then could the executive be independent. He did not trust the popular judgment and opposed popular elections, citing the fact that the people in Massachusetts had not reelected Governor James Bowdoin after he had moved actively against the Shaysites. Gerry maintained that "the evils we experience flow from an excessive democracy."[55] He did support, however, the Electoral College plan eventually adopted, probably because the state legislatures would determine how the electors were to be selected.

It was Gerry who introduced the veto provision adopted by the Convention. He did not support the absolute veto, but felt that requiring a three-fourth vote to override was cumbersome and would make an override virtually impossible. Therefore, his proposal called for a two-thirds vote to override the veto. Gerry favored impeachment of the executive on the grounds that: "A good magistrate will not fear [it]. A bad one ought to be kept in fear [of it]."[56] He was consistent in his views on the separation of powers, objecting to the inclusion of judges in the veto process. He was against including the Senate both in the appointment and treaty processes. He was opposed to the Vice Presidency and to the duties assigned to the office, as putting an executive officer at the head of a legislative house. In fact he opposed so much that he withheld his signature from the Constitution. Nevertheless, Gerry's contribution to the executive article was important.

Charles Pinckney must also be included in the list of those contributing to the Presidency. He cannot be placed in the same category as Wilson and Morris, however, in his support of a strong executive. He opposed, for example, every motion for popular election of the President. This was a litmus test of the strong executive faction. His main contribution was the executive clause in the Pinckney Plan.

Another important contributor to the Presidential article was Rufus King of Massachusetts, at 32 years of age in 1787, one of the youngest of the Framers. King was a Harvard graduate who had served in the Revolutionary War, become a lawyer, and been elected to Congress. Strongly influenced by Shays's Rebellion in Massachusetts, he had become a supporter of the nationalist element both in Congress and in the Convention. At the Convention, King generally sided with Gerry and, on several occasions, seconded Gerry's motions. He was an advocate of a strong executive even to the point of granting him an absolute veto. He preferred that the executive be elected for an indeterminate period during good behavior but, failing that, he favored a 20-year term. He also preferred election by the people, but agreed to any proposal except election by the legislature. He opposed the idea of an executive council as impinging on the secrecy, despatch, and fidelity which he considered essential to a successful executive. His longest speech in the Convention opposed impeachment of the executive by the legislature. His view was that, because the Convention had turned down tenure during good behavior, the people themselves could exercise this judgment on the President in the next election. King supported impeachment only if executive tenure was long. He served on the Committee on Remaining Matters, and the Committee of Style. Although there are no records of the proceedings of the Committee on Remaining Matters, its decisions on the executive certainly coincided with the ideas espoused by King. He signed the Constitution and supported it in the Massachusetts ratifying convention.

Alexander Hamilton is generally included among those who contributed most to the Presidential article, but, actually, Hamilton had little impact on the executive that emerged at the Convention. His greatest contribution, of course, was during the ratification process following the Convention, particularly in New York: he was the author of _Federalist Papers_ 67 through 77, which dealt with the executive. At the Constitutional Convention he was hampered by the fact that the other two New York delegates, John Lansing and Robert Yates, opposed the direction of the Convention toward formation of a national government and left on July 10. This meant that New York lacked a quorum and Hamilton, therefore, could not vote. Moreover, Hamilton's attendance was sporadic. He participated in the debate on the executive only on four occasions. On June 4 he seconded Wilson's motion to provide the executive with an absolute veto, which was resoundingly defeated by a 10-0 vote.

On June 18 Hamilton presented his plan of government in a remarkable day-long speech. The plan provided for a single executive, elected by electors, who would serve during good behavior and who could be removed through impeachment for malpractice and corruption. He would have an absolute veto; could appoint his own department heads but would share other appointments with the Senate; had a pardoning power; would be commander in chief; and could make treaties by and with the advice and consent of the Senate. Despite glowing comments about the speech, Hamilton's plan was not considered by the Convention.[57]   On September 6 he suggested that, instead of requiring a majority vote to elect the President, that a plurality should be sufficient, eliminating the contingent election feature of the electoral plan. On September 12 he disagreed with the provision for a two-thirds vote of both houses to override a Presidential veto. He still favored an absolute veto. Thus, although Hamilton supported the executive article as it was finally submitted, he contributed little to it.

Influence of George Washington

Any discussion of those Framers who were particularly influential at the Convention would be incomplete without mention of George Washington. Certainly, there was no greater supporter of the national interest than Washington. He had urged changes in the structure of Congress toward a stronger central government as early as his June 13, 1776 letter to Congress.[58] Throughout the Revolutionary War Washington urged Congress to take steps to improve the structure of government in order to make it more viable and effective. After the war, in letters to Richard Henry Lee, Madison, Henry Knox, James Duane, David Humphreys and others, Washington stressed the importance of a strong central government to ensure the survival of the nation. He feared that, if nothing were done, the prediction of the British would come true: "leave them [the Americans] to themselves, and their government will soon dissolve." Washington saw the Confederation as "fast verging to anarchy and confusion."[59] In July 1783, at war's end, he was advocating a Convention to establish a constitution to strengthen the central government. In his Circular Letter to the states at the time that he relinquished command of American forces and retired to Mount Vernon, he urged that the Articles be amended to make the government more effective.[60]

It is generally accepted that Washington's decision to attend the Convention persuaded many delegates from other states to attend. At the Convention, Washington and Franklin were the only men present who enjoyed a national reputation. In 1787 Washington was at the height of his popularity, which was reflected in the enthusiastic reception when he arrived in Philadelphia and in the continuing response of the people during his stay there. His unanimous appointment as President of the Convention is further indication of his standing among the delegates.

Although, during the Convention, Washington did not participate in the debates, and there are only four instances in which his vote as a member of the Virginia delegation was recorded, everyone present was fully aware of his support for a strong national government and a strong executive. He attended caucuses of the Virginia delegation and met with other groups and individuals where he gave his opinion on matters under discussion in the Convention. Washington's influence at these meetings cannot be proved empirically but there is no question that his reputation and the respect that others had for him strengthened his arguments.

Washington's election as President of the Convention was in itself an acknowledgment by his peers of his commanding presence. He probably had more influence on the executive article than on any other part of the Constitution. His views on the executive were well known and unquestionably influenced others. In Committee of the Whole, he voted in favor of a single executive and, later, on July 26, he joined other adherents of a strong executive in voting against the executive article as it then stood, primarily because it provided for legislative election.[61]

There can be no doubt that during the debates on the executive provisions, all of which were directed to Washington as presiding officer, the delegates assumed that he was the most logical candidate for first President. His influence on the presidential article was not a direct one occasioned by his involvement in debate. Rather, it was more powerful, because indirect -- resting on his reputation, the high regard of the delegates, and by his mere presence in the room. Pierce Butler acknowledged this influence after the Convention in writing to Weedon Butler:

> I am free to acknowledge that his powers [the President's] are full great, and greater than I was disposed to make them. Nor, _entre nous_, do I believe they would have been so great had not many of the members cast their eyes towards General Washington as President; and shaped their ideas of the powers to be given to a President by their opinions of his virtue."[62]

Even outside the Convention there was speculation that Washington would be the first President. In a letter to Timothy Pickering dated August 30, 1787, Benjamin Rush acknowledged a general sentiment: "General Washington it is said will be placed at the head of the new government." [63]

Concern within the Convention about misuse or abuse of power, and the establishment of a monarchy, was directed at the Presidency after Washington. As early as June 4, Franklin pointed out that "The first man, put at the helm, will be a good one. Nobody knows what sort may come afterwards."[64] Everyone present knew that he was referring to Washington as first

The Executive in the Constitutional Convention

President. Therefore, what the delegates did was to write an article that conformed to their high regard for Washington in the expectation that the precedents he would set while in office would ensure an effective, uncorrupted administration of government in the future.

Washington's influence extended beyond the Convention to the ratifying conventions at the state level. The one argument that the Antifederalists could not overcome or combat was the fact that Washington had presided over the Convention, had signed the Constitution, and was an avowed supporter of it.

In sum, his contributions and influence were as great as any who attended the Convention.

Thoughtful Americans have always been impressed by the thoroughness with which the delegates dealt with every aspect of government during the summer of 1787 in Philadelphia. The executive article was the one most debated in Convention and the one considered the most difficult of solution. The arguments ranged far afield at times but always addressed those important factors in the creation of an executive in a republican polity: a single or plural executive; the fear of monarchy; the importance of unity, secrecy, and despatch in the office; tenure, election and re-election; the powers, duties, and composition of the office; removal from office. A study of the debates demonstrates the practical approach of the Framers to the problem and the effect of American experience on the creation of the Presidency.

CHAPTER FOUR

The Debates

Author's Note

The thesis of this study is that the American
Presidency was created as a consequence of American
experience at the state and Confederation levels, and
through the work of hard-headed, practical, experienced politicians. Nothing makes this clearer than a
study of the debates on the executive at the Constitutional Convention.

The first of these debates was on June 1, 1787
and the last on Saturday, September 15, just two days
before the Convention adjourned. In between, executive provisions were debated during forty days.
Creating the Presidency was one of the most difficult
tasks facing the Framers. They applied to it their
practical political experience and knowledge of
government. This is clearly evident in the debates.

We are fortunate in having as complete a record
of the Convention debates as we have. There were no
verbatim minutes of the Convention. The Secretary of
the Convention kept the Journal which was a bare
recording of the resolutions introduced and the votes
taken. Several of the delegates kept informal notes
of some of the debates. But we are indebted particularly to James Madison who recorded the discussion as

79

it took place, "with a labor and exactness beyond comprehension," as Jefferson reported to John Adams.[1] In the preface of the debates which were published in 1836, Madison explained the procedure he used in recording his notes:

> I chose a seat in front of the presiding member, with the other members, on my right and left hand. In this favorable position for hearing all that passed I noted in terms legible and in abbreviations and marks intelligible to myself what was read from the Chair or spoken by the members; and losing not a moment unnecessarily between the adjournment and reassembling of the Convention I was enabled to write out my daily notes during the session or within a few finishing days after its close.[2]

Madison's notes represent a chronological record, since they were taken as the discussions occurred. This makes it difficult for the reader to follow discussions on specific subjects. On any given day the delegates might have discussed matters pertaining to the legislature, the judiciary, and the executive without coming to any conclusion. Debate on the subject might continue on the following days or be postponed for as much as several weeks. These discussions were, of course, recorded as they occurred. In the case of the executive article, with which we are concerned, the procedure for selecting the President was discussed eighteen times in Convention; presidential tenure eleven times; the veto power eight times; and, impeachment fifteen. There were in fact eighty-seven different debates on presidential matters. In addition, the executive provision was discussed in the Committee of Detail, the Committee on Remaining Matters, and the Committee of Style. Madison made no attempt to arrange these debates by topic.

The Debates

In order for the reader to better appreciate and understand the tenor of the debates on the executive, I have presented them in topical form by breaking them down into twelve different subject categories. Each of these debates has been arranged and is presented chronologically.

It should be stressed that the debates appearing in this study are a paraphrased and edited version of Madison's notes. They are not given as Madison wrote them. Since he reported the debates as they occurred without emendations, he included many arguments that were repetitious or not germane to the issue under discussion. I have, therefore, presented only the most important and cogent arguments, being careful always to preserve the views of the speakers. Occasionally, information derived from the notes taken by other Framers is also included.

The debates on the Presidency have not been presented in this form before. My intent is to offer the modern reader an up-to-date version of these debates in a form and style to which contemporary students and laymen can relate.

The categories in which the debates are divided for purposes of this study are:

Debate on the Single Executive.
Debate on an Executive Council.
Debate on Presidential Selection.
Debate on Presidential Tenure and Reelection.
Debate on Impeachment.
Debate on General Powers and Duties.
Debate on the Appointing Power.
Debate on the Treaty-Making Power.
Debate on the Pardoning Power.
Debate on the Commander in Chief.
Debate on the Veto Power.
Debate on Succession and the Vice Presidency.

The Constitutional Executive

On Friday, June 1, the Committee of the Whole began consideration of Resolution 7 of the Virginia Plan which dealt with the executive:

> Resolved that a National Executive be instituted: to be chosen by the National Legislature for the term of   years, to receive punctually at stated times, a fixed compensation for the services rendered, in which no increase or diminution shall be made so as to affect the Magistracy, existing at the time of increase or diminution, and to be ineligible a second time; and that besides a general authority to execute the National laws, it ought to enjoy the Executive rights vested in Congress by the Confederation.[3]

Like the rest of the Virginia Plan, this resolution was general and open to discussion and amendment.

The resolution reflects the experiences at the state level in that it provides for a fixed compensation and denies the executive a second term. Of some importance is the provision for "a National Executive." This was a definite departure from the Articles of Confederation which had no such provision. The Convention agreed without debate to institute a national executive.[4]

. . . . . .

The Single Executive

Having resolved to create the office, the question arose as to the nature of the office -- whether there should be a single or plural executive. The resolution was silent on this matter. If the practice in most of the states was followed, the executive would be one person assisted by a privy council. Advocates of a strong executive favored the one-man executive established under the New York and Massachusetts constitutions. The Framers also had to consider the procedure followed in the Confederation, where executive functions had been discharged by committees, boards, and finally department heads, all appointed by Congress. The experiences within the states, and in the Confederation, would have an influence on the debate. Many of the arguments for and against a single executive that would be advanced had been used previously, especially when the state constitutions were being formed.

James Wilson of Pennsylvania opened the debate by introducing a motion that the executive "consist of a single person." The motion was seconded by Charles Pinckney of South Carolina.[5]

There was "a considerable pause" among the delegates and Nathaniel Gorham of Massachusetts, Chairman of the Committee of the Whole, stated that if there was to be no discussion he would put the question. Benjamin Franklin, however, wanted discussion on a subject which he felt was "a point of great importance."[6]

Wilson stressed the importance of secrecy, vigor, dispatch, and responsibility as essential requirements in an executive and emphasized that these qualities could best be found in a single executive.[7]

Roger Sherman of Connecticut opposed the motion. He felt that the composition of the executive should be determined by the national legislature as the "best judges of the business which ought to be done by the executive department, and consequently the number necessary from time to time for doing it." Sherman was advocating the method provided in the Articles of Confederation.[8]

The Constitutional Executive

Edmund Randolph of Virginia introduced the most telling argument against a single executive, and one which reflected the republican polity of the day. He was Governor of Virginia under a constitution which severely limited the powers of the executive and provided that he act in concert with a Council. A single executive, in his view, was aping the British king. It was the "foetus of monarchy." He favored a three-man executive. He saw no reason why the requisites advanced by Wilson could not be filled by such an executive structure, while at the same time avoiding the risk of monarchy. He pointed out that there would be greater independence in a three-man executive because it would be more difficult to adversely influence three men than one.[9]

James Madison interjected that the best plan would probably be a single executive assisted by a council serving in a purely advisory capacity. He was supported by Elbridge Gerry of Massachusetts.[10]

Randolph did not think that a council was sufficient check on an ambitious man. Hugh Williamson of North Carolina saw no difference between an executive with a council and a multiple executive.[11]

The Committee could not arrive at a decision and the matter was postponed. On the following day, the motion for a single executive was reintroduced, and again strenuously opposed by Randolph. He suggested that there be three executives selected from different parts of the country, thus assuring representation of all viewpoints.[12]

Pierce Butler of South Carolina was opposed to a three-man executive as leading to divided authority.[13]

Wilson pointed out that each of the thirteen states had agreed to a single executive and none had considered three heads of state. Three executives would lead to dissension and "uncontrolled, continued and violent animosities."[14]

Sherman reminded the delegates that the states had provided a council to assist the executive. He thought that a single executive would be more acceptable to the people if there was such a council attached to him.[15]

Williamson then asked Wilson if he intended to have a council, and Wilson replied that he was against it since a council more often than not was a cover for malpractice.[16]

Gerry then attacked Randolph's idea as tantamount to "a general with three heads."[17]

The question was put to the Committee which voted 7 to 3 for a single executive.[18]

The voting within the Virginia delegation is of particular interest since it is the first time that Washington's vote is noted. He supported the motion.[19]

George Mason of Virginia still opposed a single executive as laying the groundwork for an elective monarchy which would eventually become an hereditary one. He favored the Randolph concept of three executives from different parts of the country.[20]

This prompted Benjamin Franklin to join the debate. He agreed with Randolph and Mason that a single executive would always look toward increasing his powers, and that would eventually produce a monarchy.[21]

Wilson's last word on the subject was on June 16. He again stressed that one man would be more responsible than three. He emphasized that "in order to control the legislative authority you must divide it. In order to control the executive you must unite it."[22]

Even after the Convention had unanimously agreed to the motion, Hugh Williamson continued to voice his dislike of the single executive provision. He supported Randolph's plan, pointing out that, since each section of the country was different and had different interests, each section should be represented in the executive office. He was concerned that the Convention had in effect agreed to an "elective king" who would be succeeded by his children. In his view, it was inevitable that a monarchy would eventually be established, but he wanted to put off the day as long as possible.[23] Despite Williamson's objections the question was not taken up again.

In summary, there was surprisingly little disagreement on the establishment of a single executive. Five members participating in the debate objected to the provision, and, one of these, Sherman, changed his mind. The single executive provision was agreed to as early as June 4, and was never seriously challenged after that. The vote in favor was 7 to 3 with only New York, Delaware, and Maryland voting against it. None of these states participated in the debate.

Wilson's main focus was that a one-man executive would provide greater independence, secrecy, vigor, dispatch, efficiency, and responsibility.

The two main arguments advanced against the single executive dwelt on the fear of establishing a monarchy, and the need for adequate representation in the executive office of all parts of the country.

. . . . . .

The Debate On An Executive Council

During the debate on the composition of the executive there had been references made to the advisability of establishing an executive council. Such councils had been used during the colonial period, and all but three of the state constitutions provided for them.

There was no debate on a council in Committee of the Whole. On August 18, the Convention took up the matter at the prompting of Oliver Ellsworth of Connecticut. He favored a council solely to advise the President. It would consist of the heads of the executive departments, the President of the Senate, and the Chief Justice of the Supreme Court.[24]

Pinckney felt that the President should be able to seek advice or not as he chose. He remarked: "Give him an able council, and it will thwart him; a weak one and he will shelter himself under their sanction."[25]

Gerry opposed including department heads and the Chief Justice in a council since they had other duties to perform, and John Dickinson did not think department heads should form part of the council if they were appointed by the executive.[26]

Two days later, on August 20, Gouverneur Morris of Pennsylvania introduced a proposal for a Council of State "to assist the President in conducting public affairs." The matter was turned over to the Committee of Detail for their study. On August 22, that Committee recommended approval. On August 31, it was referred to the Committee on Remaining Matters. That committee rejected the idea, and proposed, instead, that the President be authorized to require opinions in writing from executive department heads.[27]

On September 7, Mason voiced his disappointment over the fact that an executive council had been rejected, pointing out that even "the Grand Signor himself had his Divan." He moved that the Committee on Remaining Matters be instructed to prepare a clause establishing a Privy Council consisting of six members chosen from three sections of the country.[28]

Franklin seconded the motion. He thought "a council would not only be a check on a bad President but be a relief to a good one."[29]

Morris reported that the Committee on Remaining Matters (of which he was a member) rejected a council because a President might persuade the council to support him on wrong measures.[30]

Wilson favored a council if the President was not bound to follow its advice. Dickinson supported the proposal, as did Madison, but the motion was defeated 8 to 3. The Convention did approve the clause whereby the President could call for written opinions from department heads.[31]

Mason was still not satisfied. In his speech explaining why he could not sign the Constitution, he gave as one of his reasons, the fact that no council had been established for the President: "a thing unknown in any safe and regular government."[32]

. . . . . .

Debate On Presidential Selection

The thorniest problem confronting the Framers was the manner of selecting an executive. Wilson considered it to be "the most difficult of all on which we have had to decide."[33]

The executives in eight of the states were appointed by the legislature. In New York and the four New England states, the governors were elected mediately or immediately by the people. Resolution No. 7 of the Virginia Plan called for the executive to be "chosen by the national legislature."

The main debate was between the advocates of a strong executive and those who continued to believe in the omnipotence of the legislature. The first group insisted on the independence of the executive, which they felt could only be achieved by some form of popular election. This faction consisted primarily of Wilson, Morris, King, Madison, Dickinson, Carroll, Paterson, and Hamilton. The opposition came mainly from Sherman, Rutledge, Pinckney, Williamson, Houston, Spaight, Mason, and Randolph. Although the first group consisted mainly of northerners, and the opposition were mostly southerners, geography or differing economic interests do not seem to have been determinants. A third group, consisting of Gerry, Martin, Broom, Butler, and Ellsworth, favored greater involvement by the states in the selection process.

During the course of the debate, selection was also tied to the large state-small state controversy on representation. The smaller states favored appointment by the legislature in such a manner as would give them greater input in selecting the President. In the long run, the issue was narrowed to the matter of executive independence versus the insistence by the smaller states on more influence in the selection of the executive. The electoral college plan which emerged from the Committee on Remaining Matters addressed itself to this issue. It was one of the most important compromises agreed to by the delegates.

The debate commenced on June 1 and was not resolved until September 7. The question was also referred to the Committee of Detail, and to the Committee on Remaining Matters. Few, if any, subjects aroused as much interest. Twenty-six of the delegates are recorded as having participated in the debate. There were a total of thirty-two votes taken.

Wilson opened the debate somewhat hesitantly fearing that his ideas might be considered unrealistic. He favored a popular election as in New York and Massachusetts where it had proven to be effective.[34]

Sherman insisted that the legislature appoint the executive. The executive should be "absolutely dependent" on that body, because his duty was merely to discharge the will of the legislature. If the executive was made independent of the legislature it might lead to tyranny.[35]

Wilson disagreed. He wanted the executive and both houses to be completely independent of each other. This could best be achieved if they were all elected by the people.[36]

Although no decision was reached the issue was joined on the first day of debate -- the independence of the executive versus the omnipotence of the legislature.

On June 2, Wilson submitted a resolution providing for election by electors chosen by the people in separate election districts within each state. This was the genesis of the electoral college system.[37]

Gerry supported Wilson in principle. He opposed appointment by the legislature as bringing on "constant intrigue" between the executive and the legislature. However, he would not involve the people in the election, because they were too ill-informed.[38]

Williamson disagreed with the proposal and favored legislative appointment.[39]

Wilson's motion was defeated by 8 to 2 and appointment by the national legislature agreed upon by the same margin.[40]

Thus, as early as the second day of debate the Committee of the Whole had decided on legislative appointment.

On June 9, Gerry indicated his opposition to the method that had been agreed upon, and suggested that election be by the state executives. Randolph objected primarily because such an appointee would be too "partial to the interests of the state" and less likely to advance national interests. The motion was defeated by a 10 to 0 vote.[41]

On July 17, Morris charged that legislative appointment made the executive "the mere creature of the legislature." His selection would be the "the work of intrigue, of cabal, and of faction." He wanted a popular election as in New York and Connecticut. He moved that the executive be elected by the "citizens of the United States"[42]

Sherman of Connecticut raised the small state argument for the first time. Election by the people meant that the large states would dominate the election.[43]

Wilson supported the motion. He reiterated his arguments that legislative appointment would lead to executive dependence on the legislature.[44]

Mason thought the country too large for the people to be sufficiently informed to make the right decision. He considered it "as unnatural to refer the choice of a proper character for chief magistrate to the people, as it would to refer a trial of colors to a blind man."[45]

Williamson concurred. Election by the people was tantamount to election by lot and would lead to election of someone from a large state.[46]

The motion for a popular election was defeated by a 9 to 1 vote.[47]

Luther Martin of Maryland introduced a motion for election by electors appointed by the state legislatures. Broom of Delaware seconded the motion. It was defeated 8 to 2.[48]

The Convention then voted unanimously to accept the recommendation of the Committee of the Whole that the executive be appointed by the national legislature.[49]

On July 19, Rufus King reintroduced the Wilson plan of election by electors chosen by the people.[50]

William Paterson of New Jersey agreed. He proposed that electors be allocated so that the smallest state would have at least one, and the largest no more than three, electors.[51]

Madison supported the motion. His main consideration was to make the executive independent, and therefore the legislature should not be the appointing authority. He was convinced that legislative appointment would be "attended with intrigues and contentions" which would be "dangerous to public liberty." He preferred a popular election, but supported the motion as a practical alternative.[52]

Gerry opposed a popular election on the grounds that the people were too "uninformed" and liable to be "misled" by "designing men," as had been the case in Massachusetts and New Hampshire when Governors Bowdoin and Sullivan were not reelected.[53]

Oliver Ellsworth of Connecticut moved that the executive be elected by electors appointed by the state legislatures on a specified ratio. Broom seconded the motion. Gerry supported it.[54]

Two votes were taken at this time. One provided for election through the intermediary of electors and that passed by a 6 to 3 vote. The other provided that the electors be appointed by the state legislatures and it passed by an 8 to 2 vote.[55]

The Convention had rejected appointment by the legislature and substituted an electoral plan.

William Houston of Georgia, and Richard Spaight of North Carolina, were not satisfied with the decision of the Convention and on July 24, they moved to reinstate legislative appointment.[56]

Caleb Strong of Massachusetts, and Williamson of North Carolina, supported the motion. Gerry, was against it. He suggested that the state legislatures elect the executive and if a majority vote was not attained that the House of Representatives choose two of the top four candidates, and the Senate would then choose an executive from those two men. King seconded the motion which was defeated.[57]

A modified version of Gerry's idea would be included in the contingent election feature of the electoral system which was eventually adopted.

Houston's motion for appointment by the national legislature passed by a 7 to 4 vote.[58] The Convention had now come full circle reinstituting election by the legislature as provided under the Virginia Plan.

Wilson suggested that the election be by a small number of national legislators drawn by lot who would vote immediately. This would reduce the possibility of intrigue.[59]

Morris was so intent on executive independence that he thought that Wilson's idea should be considered. Gerry was against any mode of election involving the national legislature. King thought "we ought to be governed by reason, not by chance."[60]

No action was taken on Wilson's motion.

On July 25, Madison introduced a new element into the discussion by pointing out the possibility of foreign intervention in the selection of an executive. This had occurred in Poland and Germany. He felt that the national legislature and also state executives could be subject to such pressures.[61]

Although he was in favor of legislative appointment, Mason considered the argument about possible foreign influence to be the most serious objection raised against such a method of selection.[62]

Butler agreed that such influence could not be avoided if election was by the legislature, but he was also against popular election as being too "complex and unwieldy." He was in favor of election by electors chosen by state legislatures but on an equal basis throughout the Union.[63]

Williamson acknowledged that legislative appointment could lead to undue foreign influence. His main objection to a popular election was the disadvantage to the smaller states. He suggested that this objection might be removed by providing that each person vote for three candidates. Presumably, one would be from his state, but the others from other states.[64]

Morris liked the idea, and suggested that instead of three that each person vote for two candidates one of which should not be from his own state.[65] (This would become part of the compromise that would be worked out to satisfy the small state interests).

Madison thought it was a worthwhile suggestion, but Gerry was still opposed to a popular election.[66]

Dickinson pointed out that "insuperable objections lay against election of the executive by the national legislature" and the same applied to the state legislatures or the state executives. A popular election was the only alternative.[67]

On July 26, a vote was taken on the entire executive article, including selection by the national legislature, and it passed 6 to 3.[68]

On August 24, the large state-small state argument concerning executive selection began in earnest. Rutledge moved that the election in Congress be by joint ballot of both houses. Obviously this would favor the large states since the House of Representatives would dominate. Sherman saw through this and immediately objected. Gorham, of the large state of Massachusetts, remarked that separate elections would cause too much delay and confusion. Dayton of New Jersey said he "could never agree" to joint ballot.[69]

Daniel Carroll of Maryland, who was a firm advocate of a popular election, attempted to exploit the apparent differences among the advocates of legislative appointment by moving for a popular election. Wilson seconded the motion but it was defeated 9 to 2.[70]

David Brearley of New Jersey reverted to the previous discussion by opposing the joint ballot feature. Wilson of Pennsylvania could see no objection to the larger states having a dominant vote. John Langdon, of the small state of New Hampshire, broke ranks with the small state phalanx by supporting a joint ballot. He acknowledged that it could be unfavorable to his state, but the experience with separate ballots in New Hampshire had caused great difficulties which he sought to avoid by a joint ballot. Madison supported the joint ballot provision, and when a vote was taken joint voting was approved by 7 to 4.[71]

Dayton would not give up. He proposed that each state have only one vote in the legislature when selecting the President. Brearley seconded the motion. This small state tactic was defeated 6 to 5 with New Hampshire voting against it.[72] A modified version of Dayton's proposal would eventually be part of the final compromise on Presidential selection.

Morris once again voiced his dissatisfaction with legislative appointment of the President. He moved, and Carroll seconded the motion, for election by electors chosen by the people. It was defeated by a 6 to 5 vote. That part of Morris's motion that the President "be chosen by electors" was now put as an abstract question, and it was defeated by a tie vote.[73]

On August 31, all postponed matters were turned over to the Committee on Remaining Matters. Whether by chance or design the Committee consisted of elements from each of the predominant factions which had participated in the debate on the executive article.

The Committee crafted a remarkable compromise plan that took into account the views of all elements in the debate. It provided that the election would be by electors chosen in the manner determined by each state legislature. This would be acceptable to the strong executive faction since it reduced executive dependence on the legislature and could result in involvement by the people in the election. Including the state legislatures in the process would also receive the support of the Gerry-led group which favored a federal system. The smaller states were appeased by placing the contingent election in the Senate where there was equal representation of all states. It was generally conceded that in most elections no candidate would receive a majority of the electoral vote, and, hence, the final election would be in the Senate. The large states were convinced that they would dominate selection of candidates at the state level. In effect, they would nominate the candidates to be elected by the Senate at the contingent election. The one element that would not be completely satisfied with the compromise would be those favoring legislative appointment, although the Senate was included in the important contingent election.

The Committee reported on September 4, and the delegates generally accepted the compromise, although no vote was taken on it until September 6, after three days of discussion. The vote on the electoral college plan passed by a 9 to 2 vote.[74]

During the debate, Randolph and Pinckney questioned the change in mode of election. Morris explained that it was intended to reduce the possibility of intrigue, to allow reelection of the President, to provide a proper court of impeachment, and because there was no real consensus in favor of legislative appointment. Furthermore, it was indispensable that the executive be made independent of the legislature.[75]

Mason agreed that the Committee's plan would remove the danger of cabal and corruption. He pointed out, however, that "nineteen times in twenty the President would be chosen by the Senate." He considered the Senate an improper body for the purpose, and feared possible collusion between the Senate and the sitting President running for reelection. Furthermore, by giving the Senate so much power "an aristocracy worse than an absolute monarchy would be established."[76]

Others had similar objections to Senate involvement, but proposals for a plurality election as a means of eliminating the contingent election, and for including the entire legislature in the process, all failed.[77]

On September 6 a vote was taken on the first part of the clause providing election by electors and this was passed by a 9 to 2 vote.[78]

Sherman suggested that the House of Representatives conduct the contingent election voting by state. Mason seconded the motion as reducing the "aristocratic influence" of the Senate. The motion passed by a 10 to 1 vote. It was also agreed to require a majority vote of all the states to elect the President in the House of Representatives.[79]

This was the final vote on the matter.

Throughout the debate on the selection of the President there were two paramount considerations that the Framers dealt with. One was the necessity of making the President independent of the legislature, and thus avoid the possibility of cabal, intrigue, and corruption. The other was to appease the smaller states by guaranteeing their equitable participation in the electoral process. This led to the system that was presented to the Convention by the Committee on Remaining Matters. Furthermore, once the President was freed of dependence on the legislature for his election, the Convention could resolve the matter of his tenure, eligibility for reelection, granting him the appointing and treaty-making powers, and providing for a court of impeachment.

The electoral plan also took into consideration

the difficulty of obtaining a majority vote when many candidates ran for the office, by providing for a contingent election. Holding the contingent election in the Senate was rejected, because it would aggrandize the power of the Senate. It would also lead to dependence by the executive on a relatively small body of men, as well as increasing the possibility of collusion. The large states made several attempts to have the entire legislature involved in the process but were opposed by the small states who preferred the Senate where all states had an equal vote. This problem was resolved by placing the contingent election in the House of Representatives voting by states instead of per capita.

. . . . . .

Debate On Presidential Tenure And Reelection

Deep in the American political psyche was the conviction that "where annual elections end, there slavery begins." This was part of republican polity and had been followed quite rigidly in the state constitutions. All the states had instituted one-year terms for their governors except New York, Delaware, and South Carolina. Rotation in office was also considered essential especially by the southern states. Consequently, all of the southern states and Pennsylvania, Delaware, and Maryland imposed reelection restrictions.

The Articles of Confederation also adhered to these tenets by providing that delegates to Congress should be appointed annually and could not serve more than three years in any six.

Interestingly, a one-year term for the President was never considered by the Convention. The main focus was on how tenure and reelection would affect executive independence, and this was tied to the manner of selecting the President. Generally, if selection was to be by the legislature, a longer term without re-election was preferred. If election was by the people, or by electors, a shorter term and reelection would be acceptable. The final decision on tenure and reelection was made only after the method of selection had been approved.

The Virginia Plan did not specify the length of the executive term but it specifically prohibited reelection.

The Committee of the Whole took up the question of tenure on June 1, when James Wilson moved that the blank in the Virginia Plan covering the executive's term be filled with "three years." Wilson also added that he assumed that such a short term would also permit reelection.[80] Wilson was a supporter of the executive under the New York constitution which provided for a three-year gubernatorial term and permitted reelection.

Pinckney moved for a seven-year term.[81]

Roger Sherman, the solid Whig politician from Connecticut, favored a three-year term and reelection. He pointed out that to limit the executive to one term was tantamount to "throwing out of office the men best qualified to execute its duties."[82] This was a telling argument that would be referred to more than once by other delegates.

Mason thought the shortest acceptable term which would ensure executive independence was seven years. He was against reelection because it might lead the executive to intrigue with the legislature for reappointment, and might also result in the legislature perpetuating in office individuals who were not qualified, but whom it could control.[83]

Madison opposed restricting the executive to one term.[84]

Gunning Bedford of Delaware advanced a strong argument in favor of a shorter term than seven years. He took the opposite tack from Sherman by asking the committee to consider what would happen if the country was "saddled" with an ineffective executive for such a long period. It would not be possible to remove him since the impeachment provision would cover "misfeasance only, not incapacity." Bedford supported a three-year term with reelection permitted up to nine years.[85]

The vote on Pinckney's motion for a seven-year term passed by 5 to 4.[86]

On the following day the Committee agreed without discussion to make the executive ineligible after seven years.[87]

It should be noted that this vote was taken after the Committee had decided that the national legislature would select the executive.

On July 17, William Houston of Georgia moved to strike out the clause "to be ineligible a second time." Sherman seconded the motion and Gouverneur Morris spoke in favor of it. He said that ineligibility for a second term "would destroy the great motive to good behavior" and would suggest that the executive "make hay while the sun shines." If the executive knew that he could not be reappointed he would be more likely to look after his own interests rather than those of the country. If, on the other hand, he was eligible for reappointment, he would be more apt to conduct himself in such a manner as to make his reappointment possible.[88]

A vote was taken on Houston's motion and the

clause was struck out. The executive would be eligible
for reappointment.[89]

The seven-year term was then taken up. Jacob
Broom of Delaware agreed with his colleague, Bedford,
that the country might be "saddled" with an incompe-
tent executive under a long term, especially if he
could be reappointed.[90]

Dr. James McClurg of Virginia thought that permitting reappointment by the legislature would impinge
on executive independence. He wanted the executive
appointed "during good behavior."[91]

Morris enthusiastically seconded the motion, and
Broom also supported it.[92]

Once again, the practical Sherman pointed out
that the motion was unnecessary since in effect the
executive was on good behavior as he could be reappointed: "If he behaves well he will be continued;
if otherwise, displaced on a succeeding election."[93]

Madison supported McClurg's motion as a means of
providing independence for the executive. He would not
be independent if he had to rely on the legislature
for his reappointment.[94]

Mason was against the proposal as a step toward
hereditary monarchy. He considered "an executive during good behavior as a softer name only for an executive for life."[95]

Madison countered that to thwart legislative
tyranny and the preservation of republican government,
an independent executive was necessary to check the
legislature.[96]

The motion was defeated.[97]

On July 19, Luther Martin of Maryland moved that the executive "be ineligible a second time".[98]

Morris delivered a long speech covering several areas and stressing executive independence, since he should be "the guardian of the people against legislative tyranny." He suggested a two-year term with eligibility for reelection.[99]

Randolph favored Martin's motion. [100]

King agreed with the remark made by Sherman that an effective executive should not be prevented from continuing in office. He was, therefore, against limiting the executive to a single term.[101]

At this juncture, the Convention voted election of the executive through the use of electors. This seemed to have eliminated objections to reeligibility, but Martin reintroduced his motion against a second term, and it was seconded by Williamson. The motion was defeated by 8 to 2. Then, without debate, a vote was taken to confirm the seven-year term, resulting in a narrow 5 to 3 defeat.

The Convention had once again backed away from their previous decision. As matters stood no term had been agreed to, but reelection was permitted.

King feared too short a term, but Morris, preferred a short term rather than resort to impeachment to remove an ineffective executive.[102]

Pierce Butler of South Carolina raised the practical point that frequent elections were undesirable because the two southern states were too far distant "to send electors often." Ellsworth thought frequent elections led to instability in the executive. He suggested a six-year term. Williamson agreed because frequent elections would be too expensive.[103]

The motion on the six-year term was agreed to by the near unanimous vote of 9 to 1.[104]

On July 24, the Convention reconsidered the question of electing the executive by the legislature. Gerry immediately objected that this would mean making the executive ineligible for reelection to ensure his independence.[105]

Caleb Strong pointed out that it would not be necessary to make him ineligible, since legislative elections would have intervened before his second appointment and he would, therefore, not be dependent on the same set of men who first appointed him.[106]

Williamson thought ineligibility for a second term, coupled with a long ten or twelve-year tenure, would be a workable solution.[107]

The Convention agreed to appointment by the legislature and this prompted Martin to move to reinstate ineligibility for a second term. Gerry seconded the motion.[108]

Ellsworth felt an executive would perform better if he was eligible for reelection, and "the most eminent characters" would be attracted to the office if this was permitted.[109]

Gerry thought executive independence could best be achieved by a long term of ten, fifteen, or even twenty years without eligibility for reelection. He reasoned that the longer the term the less dependence on the legislature. But King saw too many advantages in permitting reelection.[110]

Martin withdrew his motion and moved instead for an eleven-year term. Gerry suggested fifteen. This led King to suggest, sardonically, that twenty years be considered since it was "the medium life of princes."[111]

The convention had come to a deadlock on the subject. Wilson felt that the difficulties being encountered stemmed from the mode of election and was sorry that election by the legislature had been reinstated. He was so opposed to that method of selecting the executive, that he would agree to a term of any length, in order to achieve executive independence. He did agree, though, that the term should not be a fixed one, but one dependent on good behavior.[112]

Morris endorsed executive independence but was opposed to a long term. He preferred a short term with reelection permitted. He questioned whether an executive after serving fifteen years would be willing to retire. He might bring on a civil war in order to continue in office.[113]

Once again the matter was postponed.

On July 25, Pinckney sought to break the deadlock by proposing that the executive be limited to no more than six years in office out of any twelve.[114]

Mason thought it was a good solution. It was in use in Congress and also by some of the states.[115]

Gerry also saw merit in the motion, but Morris could not see how the plan would eliminate intrigue and dependence on the legislature. He contended that the only solution to the problem was some other mode of selection.[116]

Pinckney's motion was defeated.[117]

More and more, it became apparent that the question of selection impinged on the matter of tenure and reelection.

Debate on the subject was resumed the following day. Mason stated that in a republic all officers of government and especially the executive "should at fixed periods return to that mass from which they were at first taken." He moved for a seven-year term without reelection. Davie promptly seconded the motion.[118]

Franklin reflected that in a republic the executive was merely the servant and "the people their superiors and sovereigns." It was only right that after one term the executive should be returned to the people and thus "become again one of the Masters."[119]

Mason's motion was passed by a 7 to 3 vote.[120]

The executive was once again to be appointed to a seven-year term without eligibility for a second term. The entire executive article was then turned over to the Committee of Detail and the Convention adjourned for twelve days.

On August 6, the Committee of Detail included the selection clause in their draft constitution. Wisely, the delegates put off any discussion of tenure or reelection and concentrated instead on the mode of selection. No decision was made on this subject and on August 31, the entire matter was referred to the Committee on Remaining Matters.[121]

On September 4, the Committee suggested that the President be elected to a four-year term through use of electors. Since this new mode of election eliminated the main objection to reelection no limitation was placed on it.[122]

Pinckney, however, was still concerned that reelection would "endanger the public liberty." Williamson was convinced that the presidential election would actually take place at the contingent election held by the Senate and questioned whether reeligibility for a second term was so advantageous as to balance his dependence on the Senate.[123]

Morris countered that the President would not depend so much on the Senate for reelection as on his own "general good conduct" while in office.[124]

Wilson considered the new plan of election a great improvement which would permit "a discussion of the question of reeligibility on its own merits."[125]

The following day, Rutledge moved for legislative appointment to a seven-year term without reelection. But the Convention would not go along with his suggestion.

On September 6, Spaight and Williamson made a final attempt to increase the term to seven years but the motion failed by an 8 to 3 vote. They then moved for a six-year term and that was defeated. The Convention finally voted 10 to 1 for a four-year term without mention of reelection and this concluded debate on the subject.[126]

The question of presidential tenure at first appeared to be a somewhat simple problem. In fact the decision for a seven-year term was agreed to on the first day. The close 5 to 4 vote, however, seemed to herald the future difficulties the delegates would encounter.

As the summer progressed, presidential tenure and reelection became more and more intermixed with the manner of selection, and the importance of independence in the executive.

The paramount consideration was to provide for an executive department that would be part of a system of checks and balances. The delegates had read John Locke and Baron de Montesquieu on the subject, as well as John Adams' recent study of the state constitutions, in which he stressed the importance of balance. Furthermore, they had experienced at first hand at the state level how an unbridled legislature unchecked by the executive could lead to unjust legislation and legislative tyranny. Therefore, the matter of executive independence, in order to achieve balance and to provide the necessary check on the legislature, weighed very heavily on the discussion of presidential tenure.

That the delegates were greatly divided on the issue is evident by the sixteen votes taken on presidential terms of four years, six years, seven years, "good behavior," with or without reelection. Presidential terms of three, ten, and twenty years had also been mentioned in the discussions. Despite a long debate on the matter it was eventually resolved by the Committee on Remaining Matters.

The Committee proposal for an electoral system and a four-year term with no restriction on reelection met the approval of the Convention since it removed executive dependence on the legislature.

. . . . .

Debate On Presidential Impeachment

The only mention of impeachment in the Virginia Plan dealt with the duty of the Supreme Tribunal to hear and determine "impeachments of any national officers."[127]

On June 2, the Committee of the Whole had agreed that the executive would be appointed by the national legislature for seven years. John Dickinson then opened the matter of the removal of the executive by introducing a motion "that the executive be removable by the National Legislature on the request of a majority of the legislatures of individual states." He thought that there should be a plan for removal of the executive, but he was against impeachment. His colleague from Delaware, Gunning Bedford, seconded the motion.[128]

Sherman interjected that the national legislature should be able to remove the executive at pleasure.[129]

Mason agreed that there should be a provision for removing an unfit executive because of the "fallibility of those who choose as well as the corruptibility of the man chosen." But, he disagreed with Sherman, and would not make the executive "the mere creature of the legislature".[130]

Madison and Wilson were against involving the states because "such a mixture of the state authorities" was bad policy.[131]

Dickinson's motion was defeated 9 to 1.[132]

Williamson and Davie of North Carolina proposed that the executive be removeable on impeachment and conviction of "malpractice or neglect of duty." This was agreed to 6 to 4.[133]

On July 19, Gouverneur Morris, in expressing dissatisfaction with the entire executive article, considered impeachment "a dangerous part of the plan" because he would become a tool of some faction or of some demagogue. He thought the executive should be unimpeachable.[134]

This led to the first real debate on impeachment. Pinckney moved with Morris to strike out the impeachment clause of the executive article.[135]

Davie considered impeachment essential to ensure

good behavior on the part of the executive.[136]

Wilson agreed that impeachment was necessary while an executive was still in office.[137]

Morris again opposed impeachment. He was concerned about what would happen during the impeachment process. If the executive function was suspended during the procedure, it would "render the executive dependent on those who are to impeach."[138]

Mason insisted that impeachment was vital. No person should be above the law, especially one who was in a position to commit great injustices.[139]

Benjamin Franklin made the important point that impeachment was actually favorable to the executive. He indicated that if history was a criterion impeachment would seldom be used. The alternative, in the past, had been assassination, which not only deprived him of his life, but also of the opportunity to defend himself. He ended his remarks by saying:

> It would be the best way therefore to provide in the Constitution for the regular punishment of the executive when his misconduct should deserve it, and for his honorable acquittal when he should be unjustly accused.[140]

Morris conceded that corruption and other such offenses might properly be impeachable, but he wanted a clearer definition and enumeration of such offenses.[141]

Madison felt that impeachment would protect the nation from the "incapacity, negligence, or perfidy" of the executive. He did not believe that waiting until the end of his term was enough security. He pointed out that the executive might "lose his capacity" after his appointment. The executive might embezzle funds, or misuse his powers, or "betray his trust to foreign powers." Madison considered the executive as unique in government, in that a single individual would be more apt to lose his capacity to govern or yield to corruption, than would a majority or all of a legislative body. [142]

Pinckney could not see the need for impeachment and certainly not by the legislature.[143]

But Gerry pointed out that a good executive would "not fear" impeachment and "a bad one ought to be kept in fear" of it.[144]

King was adamantly opposed to impeachment as infringing on executive independence. He relied on the "vigor of the executive as a great security for the public liberties." This would be lost if he was subject to impeachment by the legislature. The executive was not serving during good behavior. He had a limited term and he would be judged by the people at the end of it. He should not be subject to "an intermediate trial" by impeachment.[145]

Randolph believed in the propriety of impeachments. A guilty person should be punished regardless of who it was. The executive would have great opportunity to abuse his power and this should be controlled.[146]

Pinckney felt that since the executive would not have unlimited power impeachment was unnecessary.[147]

Morris now admitted that the debate had changed his mind about impeachment. He could see the importance of impeachment if the executive had a long tenure. He thought grounds for impeachment should be treachery, corruption, and incapacity. But every effort should still be made to make him independent of the legislature.[148]

A vote was taken on making the executive removeable on impeachment and conviction, and it passed 8 to 2.[149]

In its draft constitution the Committee of Detail provided for "impeachment by the House of Representatives and conviction in the Supreme Court for treason, bribery, or corruption."[150]

The Committee on Remaining Matters changed the clause to provide that the Senate try all impeachments, with the Chief Justice presiding when the President was impeached. It also restricted the charges to treason and bribery.[151]

The Convention postponed further consideration of the proposal until a final decision was reached on the manner of electing the President. Once it was decided to use the electoral system the matter of impeachment was again taken up.

On September 8, Mason questioned restricting the charges to treason and bribery. He suggested "maladministration" as being more all-encompassing.[152]

Madison thought the term too vague and would be "equivalent to tenure during the pleasure of the Senate."[153]

Mason then proposed "other high crimes and misdemeanors." This was passed by an 8 to 3 vote.[154]

The term "high crimes and misdemeanors", which has been the cause of considerable controversy as to its precise meaning, was derived from British precedents and had been used in impeachments since 1376.[155]

Madison objected to the President being tried by

the Senate. This would make him too dependent on the legislature. He thought the Supreme Court should conduct the trial, or, better yet, a tribunal of which the Court would be a part.[156]

Morris considered the Senate the most trustworthy. The Court was too small a body and could be corrupted.[157]

Pinckney agreed with Madison. The President would be too dependent on the legislature. The two houses would be able to combine against him, and could "throw him out of office."[158]

Williamson thought that the Senate might be too lenient since it shared so many powers with the President. Sherman, on the other hand, objected to the Supreme Court because the President was to appoint the judges.[159]

Madison moved to strike out trial by the Senate but the Convention voted against it 9 to 2. The Convention then agreed to the entire clause by a 10 to 1 vote.[160]

This was the last debate on impeachment.

Throughout the debate the Framers were concerned with maintaining the independence of the President. Generally, they shied away from involving the legislature in the process, because the President was seen as the main bulwark to legislative tyranny, and his independence should not be compromised in any way. Some thought that the President should be unimpeachable and removeable only at the end of his term by the body that elected him.

A consensus was formed, however, that considered impeachment a viable method of removing the executive for cause. The suspicion and fear of the corruptibility of men placed in responsible positions made it imperative that there should be provisions for removal. But the Convention was careful in delineating just causes for removal. Incapacity, neglect of duty, maladministration, misconduct, treachery, embezzlement, negligence, perfidy, subversion, were considered but discarded. Treason and bribery were accepted, and finally, the catch-all phrase "other high crimes and misdemeanors" was included. In specifying causes for impeachment, the Framers deviated from the British custom, which permitted impeachments for such reasons as "giving bad advice" to the sovereign.

The Framers stressed the importance of the offense and its illegal nature, and the effect it would have on the performance of the President.

It should be pointed out that at no time was impeachment considered a weapon of the legislature. It was never intended to be used by the legislature to intimidate the President, but was an orderly process to effect the removal of a President who had misused or abused his powers, or who had committed crimes against the nation.

The ticklish part was determining who would impeach the President and who would conduct the trial. The Supreme Court was considered and rejected because its members would be appointed by the President. The legislature was also considered, but there was concern about placing such a power in legislative hands, since that body was slated to select the President. The proposal that the House impeach, with the Supreme Court conducting the trial, was made by the Committee of Detail, but was not considered by the Convention. The matter was turned over to the Committee on Remaining Matters which, after setting up the new electoral system, proposed that the House impeach and the Senate conduct the trial. The Committee actually followed British precedent. In England, the lower house impeached, and the upper house acted as the court. The Convention agreed to this procedure after the electoral college system was adopted, and executive independence assured.

. . . . . .

Debates On Presidential Powers and Duties

Article II, Sections 2 and 3 of the Constitution list the enumerated powers and duties of the President. Among these are the appointing power, treaty power, pardoning power, and his duties as commander in chief. These, and the veto power, will be dealt with as separate debates.

The other powers and duties expressly granted to the President by these sections are to require the opinion in writing of heads of departments; provide Congress with information of the State of the Union; recommend measures to Congress; on extraordinary occasions to convene both houses or either of them, and to adjourn those houses when they are in disagreement respecting adjournment; commission all officers; receive Ambassadors and other public Ministers, and "take care that the Laws be faithfully executed." In addition, Section 2 of Article II provides that "The executive power shall be vested in a President of the United States of America." These powers and duties are considered under the title General Powers and Duties.

. . . . . .

General Powers and Duties

Resolution 7 of the Virginia Plan provided that "besides a general authority to execute the National laws [the executive] ought to enjoy the executive rights vested in Congress by the Confederation."[161]

The Constitutional Executive

The executive powers in the Articles of Confederation included the right to receive ambassadors,
to enter into treaties and alliances, to appoint civil
officers, to commission officers of the armed forces,
and to direct the operations of the armed forces.
Also included in the Articles was "the sole and exclusive right and power of determining on peace and
war."[162]

General Pinckney of South Carolina opened the
debate on executive powers by expressing his concern
that among the executive powers granted to Congress
might be the power to determine peace and war. He
opposed granting such powers to the executive as it
would make him an elective monarch.[163]

His fellow South Carolinian, John Rutledge,
agreed that the executive should not be given such
powers.[164]

Wilson did not think that the prerogatives of the
British king, such as to make war and peace, were a
proper guide in defining executive powers in a republic. The power to make war and peace should properly
be lodged with the legislature. The only executive
powers were those of executing the laws and making
appointments.[165]

Madison agreed with Wilson. He moved that the
executive be given the power to carry into effect the
national laws, and to appoint to offices in cases not
otherwise provided for. Wilson seconded the motion,
which was carried.[166]

There was no further discussion of the general
powers and duties of the executive until after the
submission of the draft constitution by the Committee
of Detail on August 6. Instead of the statement that
"the executive was to carry into execution the
national laws," the Committee substituted the phrase:

"The executive power of the United States shall be vested in a single person," which was a much stronger and all-encompassing grant of executive power.[167]

The Committee also provided:

> He shall, from time to time, give information to the legislature of the state of the Union; he may recommend to their consideration such measures as he shall judge necessary, and expedient; he may convene them on extraordinary occasions. In case of disagreement between the two Houses, with regard to the time of adjournment, he may adjourn them to such time as he thinks proper; he shall take care that the laws of the United States be duly and faithfully executed; he shall commission all the officers of the United States; and shall appoint officers in all cases not otherwise provided for by this Constitution. He shall receive Ambassadors, and may correspond with the supreme Executives of the several States.[168]

The Convention agreed to these general powers and duties making only minor changes in wording. The most important of these was to make it a duty of the President to recommend measures to Congress instead of merely permitting him to do so.[169]

The Committee of Style made an important change in the wording of the vesting clause. Previously the clause read: "The Executive power of the United States shall be vested in a single person. His stile shall be, The President of the United States of America; and his title shall be, His Excellency." The Committee changed that to "The executive Power shall be vested in a President of the United States of America."

The Constitutional Executive

According to Edward S. Corwin, an eminent constitutional authority, the previous phraseology "designates the presidential office, but is less readily interpretable as a grant of power." The consensus appears to be that the Committee of Style, influenced without question by the presence on the Committee of that ardent champion of a strong Presidency, Gouverneur Morris, emphasized that this was a grant of power.[170]

. . . . . .

The Appointing Power

There was no mention of an executive appointing power in the Virginia Plan. It did provide that the national judiciary would be appointed by the legislature. This latter provision became the focus of debate.

On June 5, Wilson opposed appointment of judges by the legislature because it was too large a body and experience had shown that "intrigue, partiality, and concealment" inevitably results when such a body is involved in the appointing process. He indicated that one of the main reasons for a single executive was that he would be more responsible in making appointments.[171]

Rutledge would not give such power to one person because it was "leaning too much towards monarchy."[172]

Franklin was against both the legislature and the executive making appointments.[173]

Madison preferred the Senate as the appointing authority because it was not a large body and was "sufficiently stable and independent." He moved and Wilson seconded to strike out "appointment by the legislature." The motion passed 9 to 2.[174]

On June 13, Pinckney and Sherman moved that the judges be appointed by the legislature. Madison objected and reiterated his argument of June 5. He proposed that the Senate be the appointing authority. This was agreed to.[175]

On July 18, Gorham argued that the Senate was too large a body to be entrusted with appointments. He pointed out that in Massachusetts the judges were appointed by the executive with the advice and consent of the second branch and the experience had been good.[176]

Wilson preferred appointment by the executive and so moved. Morris seconded the motion.[177]

Martin and Sherman favored appointment by the Senate. Since its members came from every state they would be best informed as to who was best qualified.[178]

Mason said that the manner of appointing judges hinged on the mode of trying impeachments. If the judges were to be involved in that process then the executive should not be the appointing authority.[179]

Madison suggested executive appointment with concurrence of one-third of the Senate.[180]

Sherman favored the Senate because they would be better informed and also it was less likely that a candidate would intrigue with them than with the executive. Randolph concurred, as did Bedford.[181]

Gorham did not agree that the Senate would be better informed than the executive since both would have to rely on information from members of the state where the candidate resided. The executive, however, would be more responsible since he alone would be blamed for a bad appointment.[182]

The Constitutional Executive

The motion for executive appointment was defeated 6 to 2.[183]

Gorham moved for appointment by the executive with the advice and consent of the Senate. He said that the method was "ratified" by 140 years of experience in Massachusetts. If any part of the legislature was to appoint "it will be a mere piece of jobbing." Morris seconded the motion.[184]

Sherman thought it was better than an exclusive executive appointment.[185]

The motion was defeated by a tie vote.[186]

Madison moved nomination of the judges by the executive subject to disagreement by two-thirds of the Senate within a given number of days. Morris seconded the motion. The motion was debated on July 21.[187]

Pinckney preferred exclusive Senatorial appointment. Randolph, however, favored Gorham's proposal but would support the Madison motion as an improvement of the clause as it then stood. Legislative appointments were generally made for reasons other than the qualifications of candidates.[188]

Ellsworth thought the Senate best suited.[189]

Morris argued that just as it was wrong for the executive to be appointed by the legislature so also was it wrong for the judges to be appointed by that body.[190]

Gerry favored the Senate. He pointed out that the Confederation Congress had made good appointments, and the Senate would do the same.[191]

Madison said that he would accept rejection of a nomination by a majority of the Senate if two-thirds was not acceptable.[192]

The motion was defeated 6 to 3, and by a similar vote the Convention agreed to retain the clause as it stood providing appointment by the Senate.[193]

In its draft constitution the Committee of Detail included the appointment of ambassadors by the Senate.[194]

On August 14, during the debate on whether or not to restrict elected officials from holding any other office while serving in Congress or thereafter, Gerry commented that the likely offices that Senators and Congressmen would be interested in were those of ambassador or minister. If the Senate was given the power to appoint ambassadors the Senate would establish embassies to provide such positions. He did not want to "establish nurseries" for such jobs.[195]

On August 23, Morris contended that, since judges would be tried by the Senate under the impeachment proceedings, the Senate should not be in the position of filling vacancies it had created via the impeachment route. Wilson was in full agreement, but no decision was made except to add "and other public Ministers" to the appointing power.[196]

The Committee on Remaining Matters proposed that the President nominate and appoint "by and with the advice and consent of the Senate."[197]

On September 7, during a discussion of the Vice Presidency, Mason interjected that he disliked any involvement by the legislature in appointments, but he was also "averse to vest so dangerous a power in the President alone." He wanted a Privy Council established to assist the executive. He would agree to concurrence of the Senate in the appointment of ambassadors because he considered that to be legislative in nature.[198]

Wilson also objected to including the legislature in appointments. He felt that the executive must be given the power to appoint officers to execute the laws.[199]

Pinckney was against Senate involvement except in appointing ambassadors.[200]

Morris thought that presidential appointment with the concurrence of the Senate ensured responsibility.[201]

The Convention agreed to the resolution as submitted by the Committee.[202]

This concluded the debate on the appointing power.

. . . . . .

The Treaty-Making Power

The Virginia Plan made no mention of the treaty-making power, and the matter was not discussed until August 15. The draft constitution of the Committee of Detail had provided that treaties would be the law of the land and that the Senate would have the power to make them.[203]

The debate at first focused on the ratification process. If treaties were to be the law of the land, both houses should be involved in ratifying them. No decision was reached, however, and the matter was turned over to the Committee on Remaining Matters. That Committee proposed that the President be empowered to make treaties by and with the consent of two-thirds of the Senate.[204]

On September 7, the Convention commenced discussion of the treaty power. There was no objection voiced to the President's role as treaty-maker except as it pertained to treaties of peace. Madison suggested that two-thirds of the Senate be permitted to make treaties of peace without the concurrence of the President. He argued that a President might impede the peace process because of the power and prestige he derived from the war. Butler agreed and seconded the motion. He felt that it would be a safeguard against "ambitious and corrupt Presidents." He recalled the strategy of the Duke of Marlboro in prolonging a war.[205]

Gorham didn't think this was necessary, as the means of carrying on war was in the hands of the legislature.[206]

Morris stated that it was necessary for the President to concur in peace treaties because he was the "guardian of the national interests."[207]

Madison's motion was rejected 8 to 3.[208] The treaty power as proposed by the Committee on Remaining Matters, with no restrictions on treaties of peace, was accepted.

There was no further debate on the President's role in treaty-making.

. . . . . .

The Pardoning Power

The first mention of the pardoning power was in the draft constitution of the Committee of Detail which provided: "He shall have power to grant reprieves and pardons; but his pardon shall not be pleadable in bar of an impeachment."[209]

On August 25, Sherman moved that the clause be amended to grant reprieves only during the recess of the Senate, and that pardons require consent of the Senate. The motion was defeated 8 to 1.[210]

Martin wanted reprieves and pardons granted only "after conviction." He withdrew his motion, however, when Wilson pointed out that it might be necessary to grant a pardon before conviction in order to obtain evidence from an accomplice.[211]

On September 15, Randolph proposed that treason be excepted from the pardoning power because the President and his cohorts might be involved in such an act. Mason seconded the motion.[212]

Morris preferred that there be no pardon granted for treason rather than involve the legislature in the pardoning power.[213]

Wilson thought that treason should be included and that the power should be in the President's hands. If the President was involved in such an act he would be subject to impeachment and prosecution.[214]

King called attention to the fact that involving the legislature was against the doctrine of separation of powers. He considered the legislature unfit for the purpose because it was governed too much by "the passions of the moment." He recalled that during the recent rebellion in Massachusetts one assembly would have "hung all the insurgents" while the next one would have pardoned them.[215]

Madison thought it improper for the President to have the power to pardon in cases of treason. He suggested that the Senate could act as a council of advice in such cases.[216]

Randolph's motion excepting treason was defeated

8 to 1.[217] The Convention thereby granted the full
pardoning power to the President.

This ended debate on the pardoning power.

. . . . . .

Commander in Chief

Like the treaty and pardoning powers, the powers
and duties of commander in chief were so manifestly
executive functions there was no debate on where they
should be lodged. The Committee of Detail provided for
the President to be "commander in chief of the Army
and Navy of the United States, and of the Militia of
the several states."[218]

The only change made in that provision was to
require that the power extend to the militia, only
"when called into the actual service of the United
States." This was agreed to without discussion.[219]

. . . . . .

The Veto Power

Resolution 8 of the Virginia Plan provided:

That the Executive and a convenient number of the National Judiciary, ought to
compose a council of revision with authority to examine every act of the
National Legislature before it shall
operate, and every act of a particular
legislature before a Negative thereon
shall be final; and that the dissent of
the said Council shall amount to a rejection, unless the Act of the National
legislature be again passed, or that of
a particular legislature be again nega-
tived by   of the members of each
branch.[220]

This proposal was patterned after the New York constitution which provided for a Council of Revision consisting of the Governor, the Chancellor, and the Supreme Court judges.

On June 4, Gerry objected to including the judiciary in the veto process. He contended that the very nature of the judicial office, which already had a check on legislation, prohibited their involvement in policy matters. He moved that the executive alone be granted the veto power subject to legislative override. King seconded the motion.[221] Both Gerry and King were from Massachusetts which granted the governor a qualified veto.

Wilson preferred an absolute veto in the joint hands of the executive and the judiciary as protection for the executive. Otherwise the legislature would be able "at any moment [to] sink it into non-existence." He moved that Gerry's motion be amended to provide for such a veto. Hamilton seconded the motion.[222]

Franklin opposed the amendment. He recalled that the colonial governor of Pennsylvania constantly used his absolute veto to extort money. Every law passed required "a private bargain with him." He felt that such power would lead to abuses, a further increase in power, and would end up in a monarchy.[223]

Sherman agreed that the executive should be involved in revising laws, but no man should be given such absolute power.[224]

Madison noted that an absolute veto would not be well received by the people. He thought that if a proper proportion of the legislature was required to override a veto "it would answer the same purpose as an absolute veto."[225]

Wilson thought that the power would seldom be

used and that the legislature would be careful not to pass laws that would be vetoed. He felt it important that the executive be given power to defend himself.[226]

Bedford opposed any kind of revisionary power including the Council of Revision. He considered the bicameral legislature as sufficient check.[227]

The motion for an absolute veto was overwhelmingly defeated, 10 to 0. Gerry's motion providing a qualified veto for the executive was passed 8 to 2.[228]

Thus, on the first day of debate the Framers had agreed on a veto plan essentially the same as the one subsequently adopted.

On June 6, Wilson moved that the veto power be given to the executive and part of the judiciary. He wanted to reenforce the executive.[229]

Madison seconded the motion. He noted that in a republic the executive depended on merit alone, and would be constantly assailed by competitors. He would also be subject to outside influence. He, therefore, needed support. By joining the judiciary to the executive it would also enable the judiciary to defend itself against the legislature.[230]

Gerry believed that the executive would be more impartial in considering legislation. King emphasized that if responsibility was one of the main attributes of a single executive, then it would be just as applicable in the use of the veto. Pinckney was also opposed to including the judiciary.[231]

Dickinson considered responsibility as the most important property of an executive and he should exercise it alone.[232]

Wilson argued that although he should be solely responsible in exercising his executive duties, the veto power was a coordinate responsibility.[233]

The motion to include the judiciary in the veto function was defeated 8 to 3.[234]

There was no further discussion on the veto power until July 21. At that time, Wilson again proposed that the judiciary be associated in the veto process. Gorham objected, pointing out that in England the judges were not involved in the power. He felt that the executive alone should be responsible.[235]

Ellsworth heartily approved of the motion. In his opinion the judges were far more competent than the executive in judging laws.[236]

Madison repeated his previous argument that the judiciary would be given a weapon against legislative encroachments. He was not concerned that the arrangement would give too much power to either the executive or the judiciary. He saw the "real source of danger" to be "the tendency in the legislature to absorb all power into its vortex." The other departments required any defense "consistent with republican principles."[237]

Mason agreed, but Gerry was disappointed that the matter had again been introduced. He saw the object of the veto to prevent legislative encroachment on the executive.[238]

Strong objected to mixing the judiciary in the function. He contended that the power to make laws should be distinct from that of "expounding law."[239]

Morris did not think that the executive as it was constituted -- appointed by the legislature for six years and subject to impeachment -- was an effectual

check on the legislature. The greatest danger was
legislative usurpation. He doubted that even the addition of the judiciary would provide enough firm-
ness.[240]

Martin considered it dangerous to associate the
executive with the judiciary. Madison disagreed. In
order to check each department against the others "a
balance of powers and interests" must be introduced.[241]

Mason stated that defense of the executive was
not the only reason for the veto power. The power
would prevent the passage of unjust and pernicious
laws as had occurred in some of the state governments.[242]

Wilson interpreted separation of powers to require departments to act separately but on the same
object. This is what he intended by the motion.[243]

Gerry preferred an absolute veto rather than team
up the executive and the judiciary against the legislature.[244]

Morris contended that joining two departments to
prevent encroachment on each was not an improper
blending of powers under the separation doctrine.[245]

Wilson's motion was defeated 4 to 3.[246]

Debate on the matter was not resumed until August
7, when George Read of Delaware, moved for an absolute
veto. His motion was defeated by a 9 to 1 vote.[247]

On August 15, Madison introduced the novel idea
of submitting laws to both the executive and judiciary
separately. If either of them objected, two-thirds
vote of each house would be required to override the
veto. If both objected, three-fourths vote of each

house would be required to override. Wilson seconded the motion.[248]

The motion was defeated by an 8 to 3 vote.[249]

Williamson moved to change the requirement to override the presidential veto from two-thirds to three-fourths of each house. Wilson seconded the motion.

The motion passed 6 to 4.[250]

On September 12, after the Committee of Style had made its report, Williamson moved that the override provision be changed to two-thirds of each house. He admitted that he had introduced the previous motion, but upon reflection, considered that requiring three-fourths of each house to override the President's veto gave too much power to the President.[251]

Sherman agreed, indicating that the states would disapprove of the three-fourths override provision.[252]

Morris countered that in New York the two-thirds provision was found to be insufficient. Hamilton agreed that it had not been effective in New York.[253]

Gerry thought that requiring three-fourths placed too much power in the hands of a few men. The main reason for the veto was to defend the executive, but requiring three-fourths of both houses to override might impede the passage of proper laws.[254]

Pinckney agreed with Gerry.[255]

Madison stated that the two great reasons for the veto, were to defend the executive and to prevent injustice. He felt that the weakness of the two-thirds requirement was far greater than the danger of three-fourths.[256]

The Convention agreed to require two-thirds vote of each house to override the President's veto.[257]

This ended debate on the veto power.

The Convention approved of the presidential veto on the first day of debate. On three occasions it defeated proposals to include the judiciary in the process as was the case in New York. Twice it defeated proposals for an absolute veto.

The debate clearly pointed out that the Framers considered the veto power to be a protection for the executive, a defense against the passage of unjust and pernicious laws, and a check on the legislature. Including the judiciary in the process was objected to as infringing on the doctrine of separation of powers. This, in turn, led to interesting definitions of that doctrine. Madison held that a mix of the executive and the judiciary would not be contrary to the doctrine since it would provide "a balance of powers and interests". If it was improper to include the judiciary in the revisionary power then it would also be improper to permit the executive to participate in making laws. Wilson agreed that the revisionary power was a coordinate responsibility. The separation doctrine required departments to act separately, but on the same object. Morris's understanding of the doctrine was that joining two departments to check a third was not an improper blending of powers.

. . . . . .

Presidential Succession And The Vice Presidency

There was no mention of this subject in the Virginia Plan or in the debates in the Committee of the Whole. The first reference to it was in the Hamilton Plan which proposed: "On the death, resignation, or removal of the Gouverneur his authorities to be exercised by the President of the Senate till a successor be appointed."[258]

The Committee of Detail enlarged upon Hamilton's proposal:

> In case of his removal as aforesaid, death, resignation or disability to discharge the powers and duties of his office the President of the Senate shall exercise those powers and duties until another President of the United States be chosen, or until the disability of the President be removed.[259]

On August 27, while discussing other matters, several members commented on the succession clause. Morris remarked that since the President of the Senate was to succeed to the Presidency, he should not preside over impeachment proceedings. Madison was concerned that the Senate might stall in appointing a new President while the President of the Senate had the veto power. Williamson suggested it would be best if the legislature was empowered to appoint a provisional successor. Dickinson thought that the clause was too vague. He wondered what the extent of the term "disability" was and who was to be the judge of it.[260]

This was a prescient observation by Dickinson. The question of who had the right to determine "disability" of a President was not resolved until passage of the Twenty-fifth Amendment in 1967.

When the Committee on Remaining Matters presented its recommendation for presidential election, it provided that the person having the second largest number of votes would be the Vice President. He would be _ex officio_ President of the Senate, except when the Senate was sitting as a court of impeachment in the trial of the President. The Vice President was also given a tie-breaking vote in the Senate. This was approved by the Convention.[261]

On September 7, Randolph moved to add to the succession clause:

> The Legislature may declare by law what officer of the U.S. shall act as President in case of the death, resignation or disability of the President and Vice President; and such officer shall act accordingly until the time of electing a President shall arrive.[262]

Madison pointed out that this wording would prevent an "intermediate election" of a President. He moved to substitute "until such disability be removed, or a President shall be elected." Morris seconded the motion and it was agreed to.[263]

Madison's observation was the basis for the argument advanced in 1841 at the time of the death of President William Henry Harrison and the succession of John Tyler, that the Founding Fathers intended the Vice President to be the "acting President" until a new election was held.

Gerry opposed making the Vice President the President of the Senate because it would be the same as placing the President at the head of the legislature. There would be too close an intimacy between the President and Vice President. He was against a Vice President.[264]

Morris countered that if there were no provision for a Vice President, the President of the Senate would succeed, which would amount to the same thing.[265]

Sherman could see no difficulty in making the Vice President head of the Senate. If he didn't have that duty he would have no employment.[266]

Williamson didn't think a Vice President was necessary. He had been introduced only because the mode of electing a President required two to be chosen at the same time.[267]

Mason thought that to make the Vice President the President of the Senate was an encroachment on the legislature since it mixed the legislative and the executive.[268]

Despite the objections, the Convention agreed by an 8 to 2 vote to make the Vice President _ex officio_ President of the Senate.[269]

This ended debate on the presidential article.

. . . . . .

The Presidency created at the Convention was the product of American experience in the states and in the Confederation. John Dickinson said: "Experience must be our only guide",[270] and the Convention followed his admonition. Every provision of the executive article, from the title "President", to the phrase "He shall take care that the laws be faithfully executed," can be found in state constitutions or in the Articles of Confederation.[271]

As noted, the Convention debated the executive provisions on 40 different days. However, it was not until the September debates that such major areas as selection, tenure, impeachment, and the appointing and treaty powers were resolved. As late as August 31, the President, as constituted, was to be appointed by the legislature for a seven year term, and was not eligible for reelection. He had a qualified veto power and could be removed on impeachment by the House of Representatives and conviction in the Supreme Court.

He had also been granted specific administrative powers. The appointing and treaty-making powers were still in the hands of the legislature. Despite the efforts of the supporters of a strong executive, therefore, the President was still very dependent on the legislature. He was to all intents and purposes the Whig-type executive found in the majority of state governments.

But all of this changed after the submission on September 4 of the report of the Committee on Remaining Matters. After that, everything began to fall into place. The next day, the Framers accepted the electoral vote system, which resolved the question of selection as well as the matter of tenure and reelection. The Committee had reversed the decision of the Convention with respect to the appointing and treaty-making powers, and the Convention adopted their recommendation on September 7 and 8.

In the long run, Wilson's plan for the Presidency was adopted. He was the main initiator of the executive article. He proposed a single executive, elected by the people, with a three year term and reelectable. This was adopted with some modification. He opposed an executive council. He advocated the executive as the appointing authority and supported the qualified veto. The executive article submitted by the Committee of Detail as part of their draft constitution was written by Wilson, and most of its provisions can be found in the Constitution.

Throughout the debates on the Presidency, Wilson argued for the independence of the executive. He saw the essential characteristics of the office to be secrecy, vigor, dispatch, and responsibility. He considered the executive the "best safeguard against tyranny." The Wilson executive was to be the champion of the "liberties and interests of the people." The strong executive which emerged from the Convention was mainly the result of Wilson's efforts, aided by his able lieutenant, Gouverneur Morris, who was effective in debate and who contributed much to the work of the Committee on Remaining Matters and the Committee of Style.

The Convention adjourned <u>sine die</u> on September 17, after the Constitution had been signed. The Constitution was then submitted to Congress with the recommendation that it be submitted to the states for ratification.

Chapter Five

Ratifying The Presidency

The adjournment of the Convention did not end the debate on the Constitution. It was merely transferred to the individual states and placed in the hands of local politicians. Even before the Convention had adjourned there was indication that acceptance of the Constitution would not be easy. The Framers themselves were not completely satisfied with their work although they considered it the best that could be obtained under the circumstances. There was some opposition in Congress but the majority were in favor of submitting the Constitution to the states for consideration by state conventions expressly chosen for that purpose.

The Constitution was printed in newspapers throughout the country and this opened the debate between those opposed to it, the Antifederalists, and the Federalists who favored the Constitution. The debate continued for the better part of a year in newspapers, through the publication of pamphlets, in informal gatherings, and at the ratification conventions in each of the states.

The Antifederalists consisted of an assortment of interests united in opposition to so drastic a change in government as the Constitution mandated. Politicians at the state level, fearing a possible diminution of their power and influence with the emergence of a strong national government, were at the forefront of the battle. They were joined by others who were merely against the concept of a national government as being unworkable in a country as extensive as the United States. Old animosities between inland communities and those on the seaboard, as well as the rural versus urban interests, also had an effect on the debate. Generally speaking, those who lived in the interior opposed the Constitution. In New Hampshire, for example, the Federalists were forced to seek an adjournment of their convention because inland and northern towns needed convincing.[1] Some Antifederalists felt as Thomas Jefferson did, that all that was necessary was to add "three or four new articles to the good, old, and venerable fabrick," the Articles of Confederation.[2] There were some politicians, like Richard Henry Lee of Virginia, who wanted a stronger central government, but who could not accept a consolidated national government that, to their way of thinking, virtually eliminated the state governments.[3] Lee also was against intermixing power among the three branches of government rather than separating it. Many in the opposition were disappointed by the lack of a bill of rights and suggested amendments to the Constitution to correct this fault. Seldom in our history has the country been so involved for as long a period on any given subject as during the debates on the constitution.

Throughout the period there was an unprecedented proliferation of letters, essentially written by local politicians using pseudonyms, and printed in the newspapers. Linda De Pauw indicates that about 180 Federalist and 160 Antifederalist essays had appeared in New York newspapers by April 1788.[4] Although a great many of the letters and pamphlets attacked the Constitution, it was not a one-sided debate. The so-called Federalists advanced very telling arguments in their replies to the opposition. Each Antifederalist charge was met head on. Both sides would twist constitutional provisions to reenforce their own arguments. Thus, while Antifederalists complained that Senate involvement in executive functions would weaken the executive, Federalist Tench Coxe, writing as "An American Citizen," emphasized, that the "idea of patronage and influence and of personal obligation and dependence," was removed by the requirement that treaties and appointments could not be made but by the concurrence of two-thirds of the Senate.[5] There is no question that the Constitution received a thorough airing.

The first of these confrontations occurred just a week after the Convention adjourned. Governor George Clinton of New York, writing under the pseudonym "Cato," attacked the constitution on September 27, the very day that the text was first printed in New York. It had been generally assumed that he would oppose the Constitution, and, in fact, many in New York believed that the early withdrawal of two New York delegates from the Convention was at the behest of the governor. Clinton attacked all aspects of the Constitution in very blunt language. Three days later, Alexander Hamilton, writing as "Caesar," rebuked the governor for his opposition. Thereafter, every "Cato" letter was answered by Hamilton using various pseudonyms. This led to the publication of the most famous of all the tracts of the period, _The Federalist Papers_, which were published first under the pseudonym "A Citizen of New York," and then as "Publius," and appeared in Federalist and Antifederalist newspapers from October 1787 to August 1788. They were also published in book form and distributed throughout the country. In addition to answering opposition arguments Hamilton and his colleagues, James Madison and John Jay, entered into a scholarly analysis of the Constitution covering all aspects of the document. As Madison indicated in _Federalist_ No. 37, the object of the essays was "to determine clearly and fully the merits of the Constitution, and the expediency of adopting it."[6]

Like other parts of the Constitution the Presidency was subjected to criticism, although admittedly this was not the major objection to the Constitution. Many of the arguments which had been advanced at the Convention appear in Antifederalist tracts. George Mason, who led the fight against the executive article in the Virginia Convention, saw the office as "an elective monarchy." He was against a single executive, the manner of his election, his eligibility for reelection, his powers as commander in chief, the scope of his pardoning power, his involvement in treaty-making, and the lack of an executive council. He had voiced these objections at the constitutional convention.[7]

The President was perceived in Antifederalist literature as an elective king with kingly powers and prerogatives.[8] "Cato" saw the "great powers of the President, connected with his duration in office," as leading "to oppression and ruin."[9] The "Maryland Farmer" was concerned that one man rule would lead to monarchy or despotism.[10] Ralph Lowndes of South Carolina considered the executive article as "the best preparatory plan for a monarchical government."[11] William Findley, a prominent leader of Antifederalist forces in the Pennsylvania Convention, wrote as "An Officer of the Late Continental Army":

> The most important branches of the executive department are to be put into the hands of a single magistrate, who will be in fact an elective king. The military, land and naval forces are to be entirely at his disposal, and therefore should the Senate by the intrigues of foreign powers, become devoted to foreign influence, as was the case of

> late in Sweden the people will be ob-
> liged, as the Swedes have been, to seek
> their refuge in the arms of the monarch
> or President General.[12]

James Wilson attempted to diffuse this type of criticism by emphasizing that the President "had not a single privilege" annexed to him. He insisted that, "by appointing a single magistrate, we secure strength, vigor, energy and responsibility" in the executive department.[13] Pennsylvania Antifederalists, nevertheless, coined a new name for the executive by coupling the title of "President" with his powers as commander in chief and thereafter referred to him as the "President-General." This was an obvious scare tactic but quite typical of some of the approaches used.

There was a great deal of bombast and hyperbole in the Antifederalist attacks on the Presidency, but, by and large, the complaints were quite legitimate considering the polity of the period. Thomas Jefferson, for example, was very concerned over the fact that there was no limitation to presidential reelection. He pointed out in a letter to John Adams that "reason and experience prove to us that a chief magistrate, so continuable, is an officer for life."[14] At the Virginia Convention, George Mason reiterated his objections to the reelection provision that he had advanced at the Constitutional Convention. In South Carolina, a delegate to the convention complained that "you don't put the same check on [the President] that you do on your own state governor."[15] At the Virginia and North Carolina ratifying conventions, rotation in office was suggested as a possible amendment to the constitution. They recommended that the President be limited to eight years in any sixteen-year period.[16] These were certainly important concerns to Americans of the period, especially those of the South. Limited reelection and rotation in office was standard among the southern states. But even in New York, where the Governor had served for ten consecutive years at the time, and whose constitution did not limit reelection, the ratifying convention recommended that the President not be allowed to serve a third term.[17]

The Federalist argument in favor of reelection was advanced best by Charles Pinckney in a speech to the South Carolina House of Representatives on January 18, 1788. Pinckney repeated arguments used at the Constitutional Convention that the people should not be restricted from reelecting "a man whose talents, abilities, and integrity, were such as to render him the object of the general choice of his country."[18] John Adams also favored reelection. He replied to Thomas Jefferson: "You are apprehensive the President when chosen, will be chosen again and again as long as he lives. So much the better as it appears to me."[19]

A short term was an American tenet, and a very legitimate basis for complaint when one considers that all the states but three provided a one-year term for their governor. John Winthrop of Massachusetts, writing as "Agrippa," advocated that the President be chosen annually and serve but one year. He was following the Massachusetts precept that the executive term should be for one year.[20]

There was no important disagreement with the manner of electing the President.[21] The fact that the states were involved in the process was in keeping with federalism. In fact, Federalists used state participation in the election of the President, as evidence that there was no intention of dissolving the states, as some Antifederalists had charged. James Madison attempted to reassure the people that the states would continue as "constituent and essential parts of the federal government." He argued that "without the intervention of the state legislatures the President of the United States cannot be elected at all."[22] At the Pennsylvania Ratifying Convention, Wilson pointed out that the President could be "justly styled The Man Of The People" because he was elected by the different parts of the country.[23] Antifederalist Richard Henry Lee, writing as "The Federal Farmer," conceded that the election of the President was "properly secured."[24]

There were general complaints about the powers of the Presidency but few specific ones. Thomas McKean in the Pennsylvania Convention was pleased "to find that no objection has been taken to the forms and structure of the executive power." The treaty, and appointing powers were criticized primarily because of Senate involvement in the process. Surprisingly the veto power was generally accepted if not actually endorsed. John Smilie, did not object to it because "he [the President] will never be able to execute it." William Findley, however, included the veto power in his arguments against the intermixture of powers provided by the Constitution. He considered the veto as "another inconsistency," and as an invasion of legislative authority, since "no bill can become a law without his revision."[25] In New York, "Constant Reader," a supporter of the Constitution, suggested that a New York type of Council of Revision be instituted consisting of the President, Chief Justice, and Superintendent of Finance.[26] Thomas Jefferson wrote to Madison: "I like the negative given to the executive though I would have liked it better had the judiciary been associated for the purpose."[27] The Pennsylvania Minority considered the President improperly in control "over the enacting of laws" and they objected that the process for overriding the President's veto was "inadequate and unsafe."[28]

Antifederalists were very much in favor of providing the President with a council. In fact, the lack of a council and the objection to the President's close connection with the Senate, were the most serious charges advanced by the opposition. George Mason was particularly adamant about the necessity for providing an executive council. One of his main objections to the Constitution was the lack of a council.[29] John Smilie of Pennsylvania wanted the President to appoint all officers with the advice of a council. Otherwise the President would be "merely a tool of the Senate."[30] The North Carolina convention proposed that the President's Council be composed of a member from each state.[31] The Minority in the Pennsylvania Convention wanted the executive powers placed with the President and a small and independent council.[32] Elbridge Gerry thought it necessary in order to ensure that government matters be conducted with "maturity and judgment," that a privy council be appointed as had been the case in "every state of the Union," and in all "civilized nations." Gerry would place the appointing power in the hands of the President and his privy council, thus freeing the President from Senatorial influence.[33] William Findley, in the Pennsylvania Convention, stated that there should have been a council. As matters now stood "the Senate and President may make a monarchy."[34]

There was considerable concern over the powers granted to the Senate and especially those which were comingled with the executive department. Findley made this clear: "The great objection is the blending of executive and legislative power. Where they are blended, there can be no liberty." He felt that the President would be inhibited in his appointing powers by nominating only those who would be agreeable to the Senate.[35] In their dissent the Pennsylvania Minority stated that "the President-General is dangerously connected with the Senate" and this would "destroy all independence and purity in the executive department."[36] They also feared that the President would use his pardoning power to "screen from punishment the most treasonable attempts that may be made on the liberties of the people when instigated by his coadjutors in the Senate."[37] Gerry, objected to blending the executive with the legislature because he would have "an undue influence over the legislature."[38] On October 10, 1787 "The Federal Farmer" pointed out that the real executive was "the President and Senate in all transactions of any importance." He complained that the President would never be able to "effectually counteract" the Senate because "the will of so important a body will not be very easily controlled." This meant, that in such an important matter as appointing civil and military officers, it would be the Senate that would prevail. The "Farmer" was also concerned that only the President and the Senate were involved in making treaties, and, since a treaty was to be considered the law of the land, in effect the entire legislative process was placed in the hands of the President and the Senate.[39] The Pennsylvania Minority also objected to this provision and pointed out that "this great power may be exercised by the president and 10 Senators."[40] At the North Carolina Convention, Samuel Spencer objected to senatorial involvement in treaty-making and the appointive power. He felt that the President would always have to defer to the Senate.[41]

In his rebuttal to such charges, Wilson explained that "If the powers of either branch are perverted it must be with the approbation of someone in the other branch of government." He considered this to be a check by each side since neither could do "no one act by themselves."[42] The Pennsylvania Minority was unconvinced, however, and included these complaints in their published objections.

The objections to the connection of the Senate and President in treaty-making which had emerged at the Pennsylvania Convention, and which had also been stressed by other Antifederalists, prompted a reply by "Publius." Among the authors of the _Federalist_ _Papers_, John Jay had the greatest experience in foreign affairs and in treaty making. He was, therefore, assigned the task of rebutting the Antifederalist arguments. In _Federalist_ No. 64, Jay pointed out how essential it was to provide "perfect secrecy and immediate despatch" in negotiating treaties, and, that only the President had those qualities. On the other hand, it was also important that a proper check be provided the executive, and, since treaties were to be considered the law of the land, that there be legislative involvement. The branch best suited to do this was the Senate, because the long tenure in office of Senators provided them with an "accumulating experience" and "political information," as well as continuity in government, which would be "most conducive to the public good." The possibility of corruption in treaty-making was virtually removed by requiring the President to make treaties "by and with the advice and consent" of two-thirds of the Senate. The objection was considered so important that in _Federalist_ No. 75 Hamilton enlarged on Jay's essay.[43]

Despite these criticisms and Federalist response to them the executive article fared well at the ratifying conventions. Antifederalists were not as opposed to the Presidency as they were to other provisions of the Constitution. Historian Jackson Turner Main outlined the Antifederalist position with respect to the Presidency as follows:

> No objection would have been made to the creation of a stronger President with at least some measure of independence, though he would not have been granted all of the powers bestowed on him by the Constitution, and his term of office would have been limited.[44]

This attitude was apparent at the ratifying conventions. Few of the objections noted at those conventions became part of the amendments to the Constitution recommended to Congress. As noted previously, Virginia and North Carolina proposed limiting the President to serving no more than eight years in any sixteen-year period. New York would prohibit the President from taking command of the armed forces in the field; would exclude treason from the pardoning power; would establish a council to help the President in the appointing power; and would limit him to eight years in office.[45] None of these recommendations were adopted by the first Congress.

All of the states, except North Carolina and Rhode Island, had ratified the Constitution by the summer of 1788. The new government was to go into effect on March 4, 1789 when the new Congress was scheduled to meet. The Confederation Congress had set the first Wednesday in February 1789 as the date for the meeting of the electoral college in the various states. How those electors were to be selected was entirely up to the state legislatures. Connecticut, New York, New Jersey, Delaware, South Carolina and Georgia opted to have their state legislature choose the electors. The other states settled for popular election of electors although the Massachusetts legislature appointed two of its electors, and the New Hampshire legislature ended up appointing all of its electors.[46] North Carolina and Rhode Island did not vote in the first election because they had not yet ratified the Constitution. New York also did not vote in that election because the legislature could not decide on the manner of selecting the electors.

There were a total of 69 electors who met on February 4, 1789 to cast their ballots. These were submitted to Congress in time for the scheduled initial meeting of that body in New York on March 4, but a quorum could not be obtained for Congress to commence its operations until April 6. At that time, Congress discharged its duty under Article II, Section 1 of the Constitution, when Senate President John

Langdon of New Hampshire, "in the presence of the Senate and House of Representatives," opened "all the certificates," and the votes were then counted.   When Langdon completed tallying the vote he announced "to the hushed assemblage" that George Washington had been elected President by a unanimous vote, and John Adams, who had received the second highest number of votes, was Vice President.[47]

Washington's election was a foregone conclusion. Even as early as the Constitutional Convention it had been assumed that he would be the first President, and, indeed, many of the provisions of Article 2 of the Constitution were introduced with Washington in mind.   Throughout the period of ratification Washington's election as first President was taken for granted and much criticism of the office was muted because of this.

Washington's friends, knowing of his hesitancy to take on this new responsibility, urged him to do so. Hamilton wrote to him on August 13, 1788, "I take it for granted, sir, you have concluded to comply with what will no doubt be the general call of your country in relation to the new government. You will permit me to say that it is indispensable you should lend yourself to its first operations." When Washington replied that his "greatest and sole desire [was] to live and die in peace and retirement in Mount Vernon," Hamilton immediately attempted to convince Washington that the "success of the new government . . . may materially depend" on his acceptance. He reassured Washington that there would be no "imputation" of excessive ambition or repudiation of his word by taking the office. He indicated that it was "the unanimous wish of your country" that he be President.[48]

But Washington was obviously reluctant. He wrote to Lafayette in response to the latter's plea that Washington accept the Presidency, that the office "has no enticing charms, and no fascinating allurements for me."[49] This was by no means the typical political ploy used by presidential aspirants throughout American history. Washington's reluctance was a sincere one, and not unlike his acceptance of other important responsibilities as commander in chief during the Revolution, and as President of the Constitutional Convention. He informed Richard Henry Lee, who had also urged him to accept the office, that, "If I declined the task, it would be . . . [because] of a belief that some other person . . . could execute all the duties full as satisfactorily as myself."[50] He also genuinely preferred to remain at Mount Vernon overseeing the development of the estate. He informed Lafayette that "the growing love of retirement do not permit me to entertain a wish beyond that of living and dying an honest man on my own farm."[51] He considered his speech to Congress, when he relinquished the command of the army in 1783, a farewell to public service. He was concerned that seeking or accepting the Presidency would be interpreted as "levity and inconsistency" in going back on his word or that he would be accused of "rashness and ambition."[52] As was the case in all of the other responsibilities he had undertaken for the nation, Washington was concerned about his ability to discharge the duties of the office as well as the effect that his failure would have on his reputation.

Despite all of this, Washington was also most concerned about the condition of the nation and feared for its collapse. He had written Madison in 1786: "Thirteen sovereignties pulling against each other will soon bring ruin of the whole; whereas a liberal, energetic constitution, well guarded and closely watched . . . might restore us to that degree of respectability and consequence, to which we had a fair claim."[53]

His concern is understandable given his considerable investment in shaping the nation's destinies.[54]

He was arguaby the most dedicated of nationalists. He considered himself to be an American first and then a Virginian. He saw, perhaps more clearly than any other person in the country, the importance of a strong central government to the future of the nation. While commanding general he had experienced the frustrations of working under a weak central government.[55] In his Circular Letter to the states he considered as indispensable "to the existence of the United States . . . an indissoluble union of the states under one Federal head."[56] Shays's Rebellion in Massachusetts had shaken him considerably, and he was convinced that if a strong national government was not established, similar rebellions would destroy the union. At the time of that episode he wrote Madison, "what stronger evidence can be given of the want of energy in our governments than these disorders."[57] Washington was very supportive of the new Constitution. He had participated in its creation and had involved himself to some extent in achieving its ratification. Although he admitted that the Constitution had some imperfections, he was enthusiastic about what the nation was undertaking under the new system of government. He wrote Sir Edward Newenham that Americans were "nearer to perfection than any government hitherto instituted among men."[58]

These beliefs, which he held throughout the revolutionary period and thereafter, must have swayed him toward accepting the office of President. Obviously, Washington did not announce his candidacy, and under the new electoral system this was not necessary, as electors consisting of the most knowledgeable men in the country would determine who was best suited for the office. But he also did not take any steps to remove his name from consideration. He was very circumspect in all of his writings not to disclose any hint of interest, but he was realistic enough to accept his inevitable election, and he proceeded, during the last few months of 1788 and early in 1789, to set his affairs in order so that Mount Vernon would be managed as he desired during his absence.[59]

One historian has said that Washington was "neither running for office nor able to run away from it."[60] In one context, Washington could not run away from the office because of his firm conviction that the new system of government was essential for the well being of the country, and his inordinate belief that duty required him to contribute his talents. Without any doubt this was the greatest consideration. His entire adult life had been devoted to a performance of duty. He told Lee that "whensoever I shall be convinced the good of my country requires my reputation to be put in risque; regard for my own fame will not come in competition with an object of so much magnitude." He was more inclined to remain a farmer at Mount Vernon "unless a clear and insurmountable conviction should be impressed on my mind that some very disagreeable consequences must in all human probability result from the indulgence of my wishes."[61] He informed Hamilton that his acceptance would be "with a fixed and sole determination of lending whatever assistance might be in my power to promote the public weal."[62] There was never any question in his mind that he would accept the office, but he would do nothing to advance his candidacy and would await notification of his election in due course.

After tallying the electoral votes Congress called on its longtime secretary, Charles Thomson, to notify Washington of his election and he immediately departed for Mount Vernon arriving there on April 14. On his arrival Thomson formally notified Washington of his election and Washington, in turn, read his prepared speech accepting the office. Thomson remained at Mount Vernon until April 16 when the two men started out on the trip to New York where Washington was to take the oath of office.

The Constitutional Executive

The week-long trip to New York through Maryland, Delaware, Pennsylvania, and New Jersey was in itself a manifestation of the genuine respect and even veneration that Americans felt for Washington. It was an opportunity to show this affection, and Americans throughout the route demonstrated it. At every town that Washington passed through there were entourages of citizens to meet him at the outskirts and to lead him to the reception that was scheduled by the towns-people. At the final stop in New Jersey at Elizabeth-town Point, he embarked on a specially constructed barge, manned by selected New York pilots as oarsmen, and was conveyed across the Hudson to the Manhattan shore where he was met by thousands of dignitaries and plain people.

He arrived in New York on April 23 and his inauguration as President was scheduled for April 30. On the appointed day Washington took the oath of office at Federal Hall in a very emotional ceremony.

This was the final act in the creation of the Presidency. Its development would depend on the perceptions and interpretations of presidential power by incumbent Presidents and the precedents set by them.

The greatest of all presidential precedent setters was George Washington. This is not surprising since he was the first President and everything he did set a precedent for the future. The executive article in the Constitution was loosely drawn, as compared to the legislative article, and fleshing out the powers of the office was left to the future. Most especially this was left to Washington. The office was created with Washington in mind as first President. The Convention, the Ratifying Conventions, and the people at large trusted Washington implicitly and were certain that the office was in the right hands. If changes were to be made, and these were certainly contemplated, there was ample time to do so after Washington had served his terms. Thomas Jefferson said as much on March 13, 1789, in a letter to Francis Hopkins. Jefferson was still very much concerned about the President's eligibility for reelection. He wanted this provision changed, but "I would wish it not to be altered during the life of our great leader, whose executive talents are superior to those . . . of any man in the world . . . I hope we shall correct it the moment we can no longer have the same name at the helm."[63]

The success of Washington as President more than justified the trust placed in him by the people. The Presidency created at the Constitutional Convention was off to a good start under the first President.

Introduction

1.   Harry Main who wrote <u>Popular Government</u> is quoted by C. Ellis Stevens, <u>Sources of the Constitution of the United States</u>, (New York, Macmillan, 1927), 175-176, as follows: "It is tolerably clear that the mental operations through which the framers of the American Constitution passed was this: they took the King of Great Britain, went through his powers, and restrained them whenever they appeared to be excessive, or unsuited to the circumstances of the United States . . . it was George III they took for their model."

2.   Joseph Addison Warren III, <u>Origins of the American Presidency: A Study in Executive Theory.</u> Unpublished Dissertation. Michigan University, 1976.

3.   Joseph E. Kellenbach, <u>The American Chief Executive. The Presidency and the Governorship.</u> (New York, Harper & Row, 1966), 3.

4.   Charles E. Thach, Jr., <u>The Creation of the Presidency 1775-1789.</u> (Reprinted Baltimore, 1969), 169.

5.   Max Farrand, ed., <u>The Records of the Federal Convention of 1787</u> (New Haven, Yale University Press, 1974), I, 65.

6.   Richard Henry Lee letter to Charles Lee, June 29, 1779. Charles Curtis Ballough, ed., <u>The Letters of Richard Henry Lee</u> (New York, 1911-1914), I, 203. Lee complained that under the Virginia constitution the executive "is not permitted voice in legislation; he is in all things to be advised by his Privy Council, and both are by joint ballot of both houses to be chosen annually."

7.   Letter to Washington, January 24, 1786. Moncure C. Conway, ed., <u>Omitted Chapters of History: Life and Papers of Edmund Randolph</u> (1888), 60.

8.   For an excellent study of the state executives during the war see Margaret B. MacMillan, <u>The War Governors in the American Revolution.</u> (New York, 1943); Kellenbach, <u>American Chief Executive,</u> 31, states that "Developments at the state level had

helped to diminish hostility to the idea of a separate executive. Locally responsible state executives had demonstrated through direct example that the people had little to fear from an executive deprived of prerogative, limited in powers, and accountable to the people."

9.   Letter Alexander Hamilton to James Duane, September 3, 1780. Henry Cabot Lodge, ed., The Works of Alexander Hamilton, (New York, 1904), I, 209-210. Hamilton commented that "Congress is, properly, a deliberative corps, and it forgets itself when it attempts to play the executive."

10.   Merrill Jensen, The New Nation, (New York, Random House, 1950), 55.

Chapter One

1.   Oscar and Mary Handlin, eds., The Popular Sources of Political Authority, (Cambridge, Harvard Univ. Press, 1966), 43.

2.   Thomas Paine, Common Sense, in Richard Huett, ed., Basic Writings of Thomas Paine (New York, Willey Book Co., 1942), 20.

3.   Paul L. Ford, ed. The Writings of Thomas Jefferson (New York, Putnam Press, 1892-1899), I, 112.

4.   Handlin, eds., Popular Sources, 248.

5.   Benjamin Church, "An Oration on March 5, 1773." Quoted in Gordon S. Wood, The Creation of the American Republic. 1776-1787 (New York, W. W. Norton & Co. Inc., 1969), 24.

6.   Allan Nevins, The American States During and After the Revolution 1775-1789 (New York, 1969), 85.

7.   Kellenbach. Chief Executive., 3.

8.   Wood, Creation, 10, 44.

9.   David Hawke titled his book on the Pennsylvania Constitution of 1776 In the Midst of a Revolution (Philadelphia, 1961).

10.   I use the terms conservative, radical, and moderate in the generic sense as a convenient way of describing subtle differences of opinion. There was no formal designation of factions during the colonial and revolutionary periods. See Fletcher Green, Constitutional Development in the South Atlantic States (Chapel Hill, UNC Press 1930), 73; Nevins, American States, 125; For the most comprehensive treatment of the Whig science of politics and how it was accepted and interpreted in America see Wood, Creation, Chapter I; Also see Jackson Turner Main, The Sovereign States 1775-1783 (New York, New Viewpoints, 1973), 109-116, for an excellent assessment of Whig ideology; Bernard Mason, The Road to Independence, (Lexington, Ky., 1967), contains a breakdown of these factions in New York, 148-149.

11.   Green, Constitutional Development, 76.

NOTES

12.   Julian P. Boyd, ed. <u>The Papers of Thomas Jefferson</u> (Princeton, Princeton Univ. Press, 1950), I, 380.

13.   Unless otherwise noted all references to provisions of state constitutions are derived from Francis Newton Thorpe, ed., <u>The Federal and State Constitutions, Colonial Charters and Other Organic Laws</u> (Washington, 1909).

14.   Charles Francis Adams, ed., <u>The Works of John Adams</u> (Boston, 1851), IV, 305.

15.   Article XXI, Maryland Constitution of 1776. See Thorpe, III, 1686-1701.

16.   William C. Webster. "A Comparative Study", <u>Annals</u>, 80.

17   E. Wilder Spaulding, <u>His Excellency George Clinton</u> (New York, 1964), 88.

18.   J. M. Gitterman, "The Council of Appointment in New York." <u>Political Science Quarterly</u>, VII, 1892.

19.   Main, <u>Sovereign States</u>, 172-173; Mason, <u>Road to Independence</u>, 230.

20.   Article VI, Maryland Constitution of 1776. Thorpe, III, 1686-1701.

21.   Hugh M. Flick "The Council of Appointment in New York State: The First Attempt to Regulate Political Patronage, 1777-1822." <u>New York History Magazine</u>, Vol. 15, 1934, 260. Spaulding, <u>George Clinton</u>, 250.

22.   Conway, ed. <u>Omitted Chapters</u>, 60.

23.   Leslie Lipsom, <u>The American Governor from Figurehead to Leader</u> (Chicago, Univ. of Chicago Press, 1939), 14.

24.   Farrand, <u>Records</u>, II, 35.

25.   Gaillard Hunt, ed. <u>The Writings of James Madison</u> (New York, Putnam, 1900-10), V, 365-366.

26.   Letter to Iredell, August 12, 1787, quoted in Green, <u>Constitutional Development</u>, 138-139.

27.   G. J. McRae, <u>Life and Correspondence of James Iredell</u> (New York, 1858), 446.

28.   Farrand, <u>Records</u>, Vol. 2, 35.

29.   Nevins, <u>American States</u>, 504.

30.   Alexander C. Flick, ed., <u>The American Revolution in New York</u> (New York 1967), 87.

31.   John T. Morse, Jr. <u>Gouverneur Morris</u> (New York, 1898), 52.

32.   John Sharp Williams, <u>Thomas Jefferson</u>, (New York, 1967), Letter to Samuel Kerchival, July 12, 1816. Jefferson stated that the Council under the Virginia Constitution was "at best but a fifth wheel to a wagon."

33.   Farrand, <u>Records</u>, I, 21. Resolution No. 8 calls for the "Executive and a convenient number of the National Judiciary to

compose a council of revision with authority to examine every act
of the National Legislature . . . ."
34.   Handlin, <u>Popular Sources,</u> 337.
35.   <u>Ibid.</u>, 359.
36.   <u>Ibid.</u>, 362.
37.   <u>Ibid.</u>, 360.
38.   <u>Ibid.</u>
39.   <u>Ibid.</u>, 363.
40.   J. R. Pole <u>Political Representation in England and the
Origins of the American Republic.</u> (New York, St. Martin's Press,
1966), 191-192; Merrill Peterson, ed., <u>Democracy, Liberty, and
Property. The State Constitutions of the 1820s</u> (New York 1966),
3; Robert J. Taylor. <u>Construction of the Massachusetts Constitu-
tion</u> (Chapel Hill, 1961), 123; William M. Fowler, <u>The Baron of
Beacon Hill. A Biography of John Hancock</u> (Boston, 1980), 242;
Wood, <u>Creation,</u> 434.
41.   Adams, <u>Works,</u> III, 12-23.
42.   Adams, <u>Works,</u> IV, 186;   John R. Howe, <u>Changing Political Thought of John Adams</u> (Princeton, Princeton Univ. Press,
1966), 93.
43.   Quoted in Adrienne Koch, <u>Power, Morals, and the Founding Fathers.</u> (Ithaca, Cornell Univ. Press, 1961), 82.
44.   Adams, <u>Works,</u> IV, 587.
45.   Samuel Eliot Morison. "The Struggle over the Adoption
of the Constitution of Massachusetts, 1780." <u>Proceedings,</u> L
(1916-1917), 363.
46.   Handlin, <u>Popular Sources,</u> 437.
47.   <u>Ibid.</u>, 438
48.   Adams, <u>Works,</u> IV, 587.
49.   Main, <u>Sovereign States,</u> 194.
50.   For an explanation of the new concept of separation of
powers and balanced government being developed by Americans of
that day see Wood, <u>Creation,</u> 446-453.
51.   Thorpe, V, 3081-90; Robert L. Brunhouse, <u>The Counter-
Revolution in Pennsylvania 1776-1790,</u> (New York, Octagon Books,
1971), 76, 91, 170, 180.
52.   Brunhouse, <u>Counter-Revolution,</u> 122-173.
53.   <u>Ibid.</u>, 172-180.
54.   MacMillan, <u>War Governors,</u> 90.
55.   <u>Dictionary of American Biography.</u> V, 122.
56.   <u>Ibid.</u>, VII.
57.   Richard P. McCormick, <u>Experiment in Independence: New
Jersey in the Critical Period 1781-1789,</u> (New Brunswick, 1950),
165.
58.   MacMillan, <u>War Governors,</u> 228.

NOTES

59.   W. B. Stevens, <u>History of Georgia</u>, (Atlanta, 1904-1916), II, 155, 305; MacMillan, <u>War Governors</u>, 75.

60.   Edward McCrady, <u>History of South Carolina in the Revolution 1775-1780</u>, (New York, 1901), 319-320; MacMillan, 74, 76.

61.   MacMillan, <u>War Governorsm</u> 78.

62.   <u>Ibid.</u>, 106.

63.   Main, <u>Sovereign States</u>, 191.

64.   Thach, <u>Creation</u>, 52.

Chapter Two

1.   L. H. Butterfield, ed. <u>The Adams Papers</u> (Cambridge, Harvard Univ. Press, 1963) II, 125.

2.   Merrill Jensen,   <u>The Articles of Confederation</u> (Madison, 1963) 178, 261.

3.   Samuel Eliot Morison, ed., <u>Sources & Documents Illustrating The American Revolution 1764-1788</u> (New York, 1972), 183.

4.   <u>Ibid.</u>, 184.

5.   <u>Ibid.</u>

6.   Edmund Cody Burnett, <u>The Continental Congress</u> (New York, W. W. Norton & Co., 1964), 673. Burnett indicates that William Blount, of North Carolina, for example, wrote to his brother: "You know I determined when I left home if I was not President that I would return shortly;" Jennings B. Sanders, <u>The Presidency of the Continental Congress 1774-1789</u> (Gloucester, Mass. 1971), 39. Sanders points out that the states considered it an honor for one of their delegates to be elected to the office.

7.   <u>Ibid.</u>, 39.

8.   <u>Ibid.</u>, 34.

9.   <u>Ibid.</u>

10.   <u>Ibid.</u>, 37, 39, 42, 70.

11.   <u>Ibid.</u>, 33-43, 97.

12.   Jennings B. Sanders, <u>Evolution of Executive Departments of the Continental Congress 1774-1789</u> (Chapel Hill, UNC Press, 1935), 172-179.

13.   Quoted in Merrill Jensen, <u>The New Nation</u>, 361-362.

14.   George C. Wood, <u>Congressional Control of Foreign Relations During the American Revolution 1774-1789</u> (Allentown, Pa. 1919), 28-40.

15.   <u>Ibid.</u>, 57.

16.   Louis Fisher, <u>President and Congress</u>, (New York, Macmillan, 1972), 3, 10.

17.   Butterfield, ed., <u>Adams Papers</u> II, 202.

18.   Wood, <u>Congressional Control</u>, 28-40.

19. Butterfield, ed., _Adams Papers_ II, 181.

20. Burnett, _Continental Congress_, 602.

21. Hamilton to Duane, 1780, in Lodge, ed. _The Works of Alexander Hamilton_, I, 209.

22. Jay Caesar Guggenheim, "The Development of the Executive Departments," in J. Franklin Jameson, ed., _Essays on the Constitutional History of the United States in the Formative Period 1775-1789_ (Reprinted, Freeport, 1970), 121; Lloyd Milton Short, _The Development of National Administrative Organizations in the United States_ (Baltimore, 1923), 37.

23. Peter Force, ed. _American Archives_ (Washington), 5th Series, III, 1241.

24. Short, _Development_, 37-40; Guggenheimer, "Executive Departments", 125.

25. Burnett, _Continental Congress_, 489-91.

26. Short, _Development_, 51.

27. George Bancroft, _History of the Formation of the Constitution of the United States of America_ (New York, 1882), I, 285. Letter Washington to Duane, 1780; Short, _Development_, 77.

28. Letter to Robert Morris, 1780. Lodge, ed., _Works_, I, 27

29. Bancroft, _Formation_, II, 411.

30. Jack N. Rakove, _The Beginnings of National Politics_ (Baltimore, Johns Hopkins Press, 1979), 284.

31. Lynn Montross, _The Reluctant Rebels_ (New York, Barnes & Noble, 1970), 192; Guggenheim, "Executive Departments," 133.

32. Burnett, _Continental Congress_, 492.

33. _Ibid._, 515-516.

34. _Ibid._; Rakove, _National Politics_, 302.

35. _Ibid._, 312.

36. Burnett, _Continental Congress_, 517.

37. Reed to Nathaniel Greene. Quoted in Rakove, _National Politics_, 307.

38. Burnett, _Continental Congress_, 526.

39. Rakove, _National Politics_, 303.

40. _Ibid._, 198.

41. Burnett, _Continental Congress_, 529; Montross, _Reluctant Rebels_, 355.

42. Short, _Development_, 51.

43. Montross, _Reluctant Rebels_, 365.

44. Quoted in Burnett, _Continental Congress_, 583

45. Montross, _Reluctant Rebels_, 365.

46. Burnett, _Continental Congress_, 574.

47. _Ibid._, 659.

48. Fisher, _President and Congress_, 14, 86

49. Burnett, _Continental Congress_, 118.

50.   Quoted in Henry M. Wriston, _Executive Agents in American Foreign Relations_ (Dartmouth, 1929), 4.

51.   _Ibid._, 57; Samuel Flagg Bemis, _The Diplomacy of the American Revolution_ (Bloomington, Univ. Indiana Press, 1967), 32-35; Burnett, _Continental Congress_, 356-357.

52.   Montross, _Reluctant Rebels_, 314.

53.   Burnett, _Continental Congress_, 490.

54.   Adams, ed. _Works_, VII, 343, 510.

55.   Fisher, _President and Congress_, 269. He quotes Madison: "I always suspected that his (Livingston's) indifference to the place resulted in part at least from the mortifications" to which he was subjected.

56. Ruhl J. Bartlett, ed., _The Record of American Diplomacy_ (New York, Alfred Knopf, 1947), 43.

57.   _Ibid._, 43-60.

58.   Bancroft, _Formation_, I, 474.

59.   Henry P. Learned, _The President's Cabinet_ (New Haven, Yale Univ. Press, 1912), 59.

60.   Sanders, _Evolution_, 97.

61.   _Ibid._ Sanders contends that the Convention was "influenced in its consideration of an executive by the experiences of the Continental Congress."

Chapter Three

1.   Farrand, ed. _Records_, III, Resolution of Congress, February 21, 1787.

2.   Quoted in Clinton Rossiter, _1787 The Grand Convention_ (New York, MacMillan Co., 1966), 54, 55.

3.   Farrand, III, 14.

4.   _Ibid._, 586, fn2.

5.   _Ibid._, 76, letter from Paris to John Adams, August 30, 1787.

6.   _Ibid._, 33. Benjamin Rush letter to Richard Price, June 2, 1787.

7.   Personal information on the Framers obtained from Rossiter, _1787, The Grand Convention_; and William P. Murphy, _The Triumph of Nationalism_, (Chicago, Quadrangle Books, 1967).

8.   Saul K. Padover, _The Complete Madison, His Basic Writings_ (New York, Harper & Bros., 1953), 4; Andrew J. Bethea, _The Contribution of Charles Pinckney to the Formation of the American Union_ (Richmond, 1937), 28-29; Charles C. Nott, _The Mystery of the Pinckney Draught_ (New York, 1904), 249.

9.   Farrand, III, 35, Madison letter to Jefferson, June 6, 1787.

10.   *Ibid.*, 59, Manasseh Cutler Journal.

11.   *Ibid.*, 76, Jefferson letter to John Adams, August 30, 1787.

12.   *Ibid.*, 479, Jared Sparks Journal. Notes of a visit to James Madison.

13.   *Ibid.*, 75, *Pennsylvania Packet and Daily Advertiser*, August 23, 1787; 81, George Washington Diary, September 17, 1787.

14.   *Ibid.*, 409, Madison letter to Noah Webster, October 12, 1804.

15.   *Ibid.*, 532, Madison letter to Thomas S. Grimke, January 6, 1834; 536, Madison letter to W. A. Duer, June 5, 1835.

16.   *Ibid.*, I, 20-23; For complete Virginia Plan see Farrand, III, Appendix C.

17.   *Ibid.*, I, 65.

18.   *Ibid.*, 21.

19.   Morison, ed. *Sources*, 183-184.

20.   Farrand, I, 23.

21.   Nott, *Pinckney Draught*, 223.

22.   Bethea, *Contribution of Charles Pinckney*, 16-18, 28-29 Nott, *Pinckney Draught*, 249.

23.   Farrand, III, 25, George Read letter to John Dickinson, May 21, 1787.

24.   *Ibid.*, 606; Information pertaining to the Pinckney Plan is taken from the reconstructred plan found in Appendix D, 604-609.

25.   *Ibid.*

26.   Thach, *Creation*, 110-111.

27.   Farrand, I, 195. For complete New Jersey Plan see Appendix E, III, 611-616.

28.   *Ibid.*, I, 244.

29.   *Ibid.*

30.   *Ibid.*, 313.

31.   *Ibid.*, 236.

32.   *Ibid.*, II, 85.

33.   *Ibid.*, 171-172.

34.   *Ibid.*, III, 68, Letter August 12, 1787.

35.   *Ibid.*, II, 481.

36.   *Ibid.*

37.   *Ibid.*, 499.

38.   *Ibid.*, 498.

39.   *Ibid.*, 501.

40.   *Ibid.*, 500.

41.   *Ibid.*, 497, 498.

42.   *Ibid.*, 499.

43.   *Ibid.*, 498.

44.   <u>Ibid.</u>, 553.
45.   <u>Ibid.</u>, III, 420, Morris letter to Moss Kent, January 12 1815.
46.   <u>Ibid.</u>, II, 594.
47.   Donald L. Robinson, "The Inventors of the Presidency," <u>Presidential Studies Quarterly</u>, XIII, No. 1, 8.
48.   Hunt, ed., <u>James Madison, Writings</u>, II, 348.
49.   Farrand, I, 67.
50.   Thach, <u>Creation</u>, 99.
51.   Farrand, II, 29, 31.
52.   <u>Ibid.</u>, 33.
53.   <u>Ibid.</u>, 52-54.
54.   Murphy, <u>Triumph of Nationalism</u>, 123.
55.   Farrand, I, 48.
56.   <u>Ibid.</u>, II, 66.
57.   <u>Ibid.</u>, III, 617-630, Appendix F, Hamilton Plan.
58.   James Thomas Flexner, <u>George Washington and the New Nation: (1783-1793)</u>, (Boston, Little, Brown & Co., 1969), 87.
59.   Saxe Commins, ed., <u>Basic Writings of George Washington</u> (New York, 1948), 524, Letter to Madison, November 5, 1786.
60.   <u>Ibid.</u>, 490.
61.   Farrand, II, 121.
62.   <u>Ibid</u>, III, 302, Letter of May 5, 1788.
63.   <u>Ibid.</u>, IV, 75, Benjamin Rush letter to Timothy Pickering, August 30, 1787.
64.   <u>Ibid.</u>, I, 103.

Chapter Four

Debate on the Single Executive

1.   Farrand, ed., <u>Records</u>, III, 421. Letter of August 10, 1815. All references to the debates at the Convention are from Madison's Notes as edited by Farrand unless otherwise indicated. Citations from the official Journal are marked as such. Notes were also taken at the Convention by Robert Yates, Rufus King, James McHenry, William Pierce, William Paterson, Alexander Hamilton, and George Mason. These are cited through use of surname.
2.   <u>Ibid.</u>, I, Madison, xvi.
3.   <u>Ibid.</u>, 21.
4.   <u>Ibid.</u>, Journal, I, 63; Madison, 66
5.   <u>ibid.</u>, 65.
6.   <u>Ibid.</u>
7.   <u>Ibid.</u>, 65-66; King, 70.

NOTES

8.   <u>Ibid.</u>, Madison, 65; Morison, <u>Sources</u>, 183.
9.   Farrand, I, 66.
10. <u>Ibid.</u>, Pierce, 74.
11. <u>Ibid.</u>, Pierce, 74; King, 71.
12. <u>Ibid.</u>, Madison, 88.
13. <u>Ibid.</u>, 88-89.
14. <u>Ibid.</u>, 96.
15. <u>Ibid.</u>, 97.
16. <u>Ibid.</u>,
17. <u>Ibid.</u>
18. <u>Ibid.</u>
19. <u>Ibid.</u>
20. <u>Ibid.</u>, 101-102; Mason, 111-114.
21. <u>Ibid.</u>, Madison, 103.
22. <u>Ibid.</u>, Madison, 254.
23. <u>Ibid.</u>, II, 101.

Debate on an Executive Council

24. <u>Ibid.</u>, II, 328-329.
25. <u>Ibid.</u>, 329.
26. <u>Ibid.</u>
27. <u>Ibid.</u>, 342-344, 367, 481, 499.
28. <u>Ibid.</u>, 541-542.
29. <u>Ibid.</u>, 542.
30. <u>Ibid.</u>
31. <u>Ibid.</u>
32. <u>Ibid.</u>, 638.

Debate on Presidential Selection

33. Farrand, II, 501.
34. <u>Ibid.</u>, I, 68.
35. <u>Ibid.</u>
36. <u>Ibid.</u>
37. <u>Ibid.</u>, 80
38. <u>Ibid.</u>
39. <u>Ibid.</u>, 81.
40. <u>Ibid.</u>
41. <u>Ibid.</u>, 175-176.
42. <u>Ibid.</u>, II, 29.
43. <u>Ibid.</u>
44. <u>Ibid.</u>, 29-30.
45. <u>Ibid.</u>, 31.
46. <u>Ibid.</u>, 32.

47.   _Ibid._
48.   _Ibid._
49.   _Ibid._
50.   _Ibid._, 55-56.
51.   _Ibid._, 56.
52.   _Ibid._, 56-57.
53.   _Ibid._, 57.
54.   _Ibid._, 57-58.
55.   _Ibid._, 58.
56.   _Ibid._, 95, 99.
57.   _Ibid._, 100, 101.
58.   _Ibid._, 101.
59.   _Ibid._, 103.
60.   _Ibid._, 103-105, 106.
61.   _Ibid._, 109-111.
62.   _Ibid._, 112.
63.   _Ibid._
64.   _Ibid._, 113.
65.   _Ibid._
66.   _Ibid._, 114.
67.   _Ibid._
68.   _Ibid._, 121.
69.   _Ibid._, 401-402.
70.   _Ibid._, 402.
71.   _Ibid._, 402, 403
72.   _Ibid._, 403.
73.   _Ibid._, 403-404.
74.   _Ibid._, 525.
75.   _Ibid._, 500.
76.   _Ibid._, 500, 512, 515.
77.   _Ibid._, 501, 511, 512, 513.
78.   _Ibid._, 525.
79.   _Ibid._, 522, 527, 529.

Debate on Presidential Tenure and Reelection

80.   Farrand, I, 68.
81.   _Ibid._
82.   _Ibid._
83.   _Ibid._
84.   _Ibid._ Pierce, 74.
85.   _Ibid._, Madison, 68-69.
86.   _Ibid._, 69.
87.   _Ibid._, 88.
88   _Ibid._, II, 33.

89.   _Ibid._
90.   _Ibid._
91.   _Ibid._
92.   _Ibid._
93.   _Ibid._, 33-34.
94.   _Ibid._, 34-35.
95.   _Ibid._, 35.
96.   _Ibid._
97.   _Ibid._, 36.
98.   _Ibid._, 52.
99.   _Ibid._, 52-54.
100. _Ibid._, 54-55.
101. _Ibid._, 55-56.
102. _Ibid._, 58-59.
103. _Ibid._, 59.
104. _Ibid._
105. _Ibid._, 99-100.
106. _Ibid._, 100.
107. _Ibid._
108. _Ibid._, 101.
109. _Ibid._
110. _Ibid._, 102.
111. _Ibid._
112. _Ibid._
113. _Ibid._, 103-105.
114. _Ibid._, 111-112.
115. _Ibid._, 112.
116. _Ibid._, 112-113.
117. _Ibid._, 115.
118. _Ibid._, 118-120
119. _Ibid._, 120.
120. _Ibid._
121. _Ibid._, 481.
122. _Ibid._, 497-498.
123. _Ibid._, 501.
124. _Ibid._, 502.
125. _Ibid._, 501-502.
126. _Ibid._, 525.

Debate on Presidential Impeachment

127. Farrand, I, Madison. 22.
128. _Ibid._, 85.
129. _Ibid._
130. _Ibid._, 86.

131. <u>Ibid</u>.
132. <u>Ibid</u>., Journal 79.
133. <u>Ibid</u>., Madison, 88.
134. <u>Ibid</u>., Madison, 53.
135. <u>Ibid</u>., 64.
136. <u>Ibid</u>.
137. <u>Ibid</u>.
138. <u>Ibid</u>.
139. <u>Ibid</u>., 65.
140. <u>Ibid</u>.
141. <u>Ibid</u>.
142. <u>Ibid</u>.
143. <u>Ibid</u>., 66.
144. <u>Ibid</u>.
145. <u>Ibid</u>., 66-67.
146. <u>Ibid</u>., 67.
147. <u>Ibid</u>., 68.
148. <u>Ibid</u>., 68-69.
149. <u>Ibid</u>., 69.
150. <u>Ibid</u>., 186.
151. <u>Ibid</u>., II, 499.
152. <u>Ibid</u>., 550.
153. <u>Ibid</u>.
154. <u>Ibid</u>.
155. Irving Brandt, <u>Impeachment</u>, (New York, 1972) 10
156. Farrand, Madison, 551.
157. <u>Ibid</u>.
158. <u>Ibid</u>.
159. <u>Ibid</u>.
160. <u>Ibid</u>., 551, 552.

Presidential Powers And Duties

161. Farrand, I, 21.
162. Morison, <u>Sources</u>, 181.
163. Farrand, I, 65.
164. <u>Ibid</u>.
165. <u>Ibid</u>., 65-66; Pierce 74.
166. <u>Ibid</u>., Madison, 66-67.
167. Corwin, <u>The President, Office and Powers 1787-1984</u>, (NYU Press, 1984), 4, 11. Corwin contends that "if there is 'executive power' that is not granted the President in the more specific clauses of Article II," it is found in the Executive Power clause.
168. Farrand, II, 185.

169.   <u>Ibid</u>., 405.
170.   Corwin, 4, 11.

The Appointing Power

171.   Farrand, I, 119.
172.   <u>Ibid</u>.
173.   <u>Ibid</u>.
174.   <u>Ibid</u>., 120.
175.   <u>Ibid</u>., 232-233.
176.   <u>Ibid</u>., II, 41.
177.   <u>Ibid</u>.
178.   <u>Ibid</u>.
179.   <u>Ibid</u>., 41-42.
180.   <u>Ibid</u>., 42-43.
181.   <u>Ibid</u>., 43.
182.   <u>Ibid</u>.
183.   <u>Ibid</u>., 44.
184.   <u>Ibid</u>.
185.   <u>Ibid</u>.
186.   <u>Ibid</u>.
187.   <u>Ibid</u>., 44, 80-81.
188.   <u>Ibid</u>., 81.
189.   <u>Ibid</u>.
190.   <u>Ibid</u>., 82.
191.   <u>Ibid</u>.
192.   <u>Ibid</u>.
193.   <u>Ibid</u>., 83.
194.   <u>Ibid</u>., 183.
195.   <u>Ibid</u>., 285.
196.   <u>Ibid</u>., 389, 394.
197.   <u>Ibid</u>., 498.
198.   <u>Ibid</u>., 537.
199.   <u>Ibid</u>., 538-539.
200.   <u>Ibid</u>., 539.
201.   <u>Ibid</u>.
202.   <u>Ibid</u>., 540.

The Treaty-Making Power

203.   <u>Ibid</u>., II, 183.
204.   <u>Ibid</u>., 498-499.
205.   <u>Ibid</u>., 540.
206.   <u>Ibid</u>.
207.   <u>Ibid</u>., 540-541.

NOTES

208. <u>Ibid.</u>, 541.

The Pardoning Power

209. <u>Ibid.</u>, II, 185.
210. <u>Ibid.</u>, 419.
211. <u>Ibid.</u>, 426.
212. <u>Ibid.</u>, 626.
213. <u>Ibid.</u>
214. <u>Ibid.</u>
215. <u>Ibid.</u>, 626-627.
216. <u>Ibid.</u>, 627.
217. <u>Ibid.</u>

Commander in Chief

218. <u>Ibid.</u>, II, 185.
219. <u>Ibid.</u>, 426-427.

The Veto Power

220. Farrand, I, 21.
221. <u>Ibid.</u>, 97, 98.
222. <u>Ibid.</u>, 98.
223. <u>Ibid.</u>, 99, 103.
224. <u>Ibid.</u>, 99.
225. <u>Ibid.</u>, 99-100.
226. <u>Ibid.</u>, 100.
227. <u>Ibid.</u>, 100-101.
228. <u>Ibid.</u>, 103, 104.
229. <u>Ibid.</u>, 138.
230. <u>Ibid.</u>, 138-139.
231. <u>Ibid.</u>, 139.
232. <u>Ibid.</u>, 140.
233. <u>Ibid.</u>
234. <u>Ibid.</u>
235. <u>Ibid.</u>, II, 73.
236. <u>Ibid.</u>, 73-74.
237. <u>Ibid.</u>, 74.
238. <u>Ibid.</u>
239. <u>Ibid.</u>, 75.
240. <u>Ibid.</u>, 76.
241. <u>Ibid.</u>, 76-77.
242. <u>Ibid.</u>, 78.
243. <u>Ibid.</u>

244. *Ibid*.
245. *Ibid*., 78-79.
246. *Ibid*., 80.
247. *Ibid*., 200.
248. *Ibid*., 298.
249. *Ibid*.
250. *Ibid*., 301.
251. *Ibid*., 585.
252. *Ibid*.
253. *Ibid*.
254. *Ibid*., 586.
255. *Ibid*.
256. *Ibid*., 587.
257. *Ibid*.

Presidential Succession And The Vice Presidency

258. Farrand, I, 292.
259. *Ibid*., II, 186.
260. *Ibid*., 427.
261. *Ibid*., 497-498.
262. *Ibid*., 535.
263. *Ibid*.
264. *Ibid*., 536-537.
265. *Ibid*., 537.
266. *Ibid*.
267. *Ibid*.
268. *Ibid*.
269. *Ibid*., 538.
270. *Ibid*., 278.
271. Breckenridge Long, *Genesis of the Constitution of the United States* (New York, 1926), Appendix, 229-231. Long compares the provisions of the Constitution with other American documents, i.e. state constitutions, Articles of Confederation, etc., to show the derivation of those provisions. The title "President" was derived from the New Hampshire, South Carolina, Pennsylvania, and Delaware constitutions, as well as the Articles of Confederation. The Vice Presidency and the succession clause can be traced to the New York constitution. The commander in chief clause is found in the New York, Massachusetts, Georgia, and Pennsylvania constitutions. Reprieves and pardons are included in the New York constitution. The treaty provision and power to appoint ambassadors can be traced to the Articles of Confederation. Electors were used in Connecticut and Rhode Island. The provisions of Article II, Section 3 which include executive involvement in the

legislature, the "take care" clause, and the power to commission officers comes from the New York constitution. The veto power was taken from the Massachusetts constitution.

Chapter Five

1.   John Langdon to Rufus King, February 23, 1788, in Joseph B. Walker, A History of the New Hampshire Convention (Boston, 1888), 29.

2.   Thomas Jefferson to John Adams, November 13, 1787, in Lester J. Cappon, ed., The Adams-Jefferson Letters (Chapel Hill, UNC Press, 1959), 212.

3.   Leuchtenberg and Wishy, eds., Empire and Nation, xv.

4.   Linda G. De Pauw, The Eleventh Pillar (Ithaca, Cornell Univ. Press, 1966), 98-99.

5.   Merrill Jensen, ed., The Documentary History of the Ratification of the Constitution (Madison, 1976), II, 141.

6.   Roy P. Fairfield, ed., The Federalist Papers (Baltimore, Johns Hopkins Press, 1981), 99.

7.   Kellenbach, American Chief Executive, 65.

8.   Jackson Turner Main, The Antifederalists (New York, W. W. Norton & Co., 1961), 141-142; Jensen Documentary History, II, 212.

9.   Letter V, New York Journal, November 11, 1787 in W. B. Allen and Gordon Lloyd, eds., The Essential Antifederalist (New York, Univ. Press of America, 1985), 159.

10.   Ibid., 261.

11.   Kellenbach, American Chief Executive, 65.

12.   Jensen, Documentary History, II, 212.

13.   Ibid., 495, 579.

14.   Cappon, Letters, 212.

15.   Quoted in Main, Antifederalists, 140-141.

16.   C. C. Tansill,   ed., Documents Illustrative of the Formation of the Union of the American States, House Document 398, 69th Congress (1927). American Studies Bulletin 10 (1965), Legislative Reference Series, 1032, 1041, 1049.

17.   De Pauw, Eleventh Pillar, 300.

18.   Farrand, Records, III, 255-256.

19.   John Adams to Thomas Jefferson, December 6, 1787, in Cappon, Letters, 213.

20.   Allen and Lloyd, eds., Essential Antifederalist, 46.

21.   Main, Antifederalists, 139-140. Main points out that "less than a dozen Antifederalist writers registered a protest against the electoral college."

22.   Fairfield, Federalist No. 45, 135.

23.   Jensen, _Documentary History_, II, 452, 566-567.
24.   Leuchtenberg and Wishy, eds., _Empire and Nation_, 107.
25.   Jensen, _Documentary History_, II, 412, 461, 465, 505.
26.   Clarence E. Miner, _Ratification of the Federal Constitution by the State of New York_ (New York, 1968), 68.
27.   Adrienne Koch, _Jefferson_ (Englewood Cliffs, 1971) 37-40
28.   Allen and Lloyd, _Essential Antifederalist_, 62.
29.   Kellenbach, _American Chief Executive_, 65.
30.   Jensen, _Documentary History_, 598.
31.   Louise Key Trenholme, _The Ratification of the Federal Constitution in North Carolina_ (New York, 1932), 172.
32.   John Bach McMaster and Frederick D. Stone, _Pennsylvania and the Federal Constitution 1787-1788_ (Philadelphia, 1942, Reprinted 1970), II, 477; Allen and Lloyd, _Essential Antifederalist_, 54.
33.   Letter to Randolph, October 16, 1787 in Allen and Lloyd _Essential Antifederalist_, 26.
34.   Jensen, _Documentary History_, 587.
35.   _Ibid._, 512-513.
36.   Allen and Lloyd, _Essential Antifederalist_, 66.
37.   _Ibid._, 65, 66.
38.   _Ibid._, 21.
39.   Leuchtenberg and Wishy, eds., _Empire and Nation_, 107.
40.   Allen and Lloyd, _Essential Antifederalist_, 65.
41.   Trenholme, _North Carolina_, 172.
42.   McMaster and Stone, _Pennsylvania_, 327; Jensen, _Documentary History_, II, 480.
43.   Fairfield, _Federalist Papers_, 187-192; 221-225.
44.   Main, _Antifederalists_, 184.
45.   De Pauw, _Eleventh Pillar_, Appendix B, 300.
46.   Neal R. Peirce, _The People's President_ (New York, 1968) 60.
47.   Alvin M. Josephy, Jr. _The Congress of the United States_ (New York, 1975), 26.
48.   Arthur M. Schlesinger, Jr., ed., _The Coming to Power_ (New York, Chelsea House, 1972; Flexner, _Washington_, 133; Mary-Jo Kline, ed., _Alexander Hamilton_ (New York, 1973), 209-210.
49.   Letter to Lafayette, April 28, 1789 Cummins, _Basic Writings_, 544.
50.   Letter to Lee, September 22, 1788. Cummins, _Basic Writings_, 548-549.
51.   Letter to Lafayette, April 28, 1788. Cummins, _Basic Writings_, 544.
52.   Flexner, _Washington_, 159.
53.   Letter to Madison, November 5, 1786 Cummins, _Basic_

Writings, 524.

54. Rexford Tugwell, _How They Became President_ (New York, Simon & Schuster, 1964), 27.

55. Fisher, _President and Congress_, 254.

56. Cummins, _Basic Writings_, 490.

57. Letter to Madison, November 5, 1786 Cummins _Basic Writings_, 524.

58. Quoted in Flexner, _Washington_, 159.

59. _Ibid._, 162.

60. Schlesinger, _Coming to Power_, 10.

61. Letter to Richard Henry Lee, September 22, 1788. Cummins, _Basic Writings_, 550.

62. Letter to Hamilton, October 3, 1788 Cummins, _Basic Writings_, 554.

63. John D. Lewis, _Antifederalists Vs. Federalists_ (San Francisco, 1961), 122; Caleb Perry Patterson, _The Constitutional Principles of Thomas Jefferson_ (Gloucester, 1967), 39.

Selective Bibliography

Documents and Contemporary Writings

Adams, Charles Francis, ed., The Works of John Adams, (Boston, 1851).

Allen, W. B. and Gordon Lloyd, eds., The Essential Antifederalist (Lanham, Md., Univ. Press of America, 1985).

Ballough, Charles Curtis, ed., The Letters of Richard Henry Lee, (New York, 1911-1914).

Bartlett, J. R. ed., The Records of the Colony and State of Rhode Island (Providence, 1865).

Bartlett, Ruhl J., ed., The Record of American Diplomacy (New York, Alfred Knopf, 1967).

Bouton, Nathaniel, et al, eds., The Provincial and State Papers of New Hampshire (Concord, 1867-1943).

Boyd, Julian P., ed., The Papers of Thomas Jefferson, (Princeton, Princeton Univ. Press, 1950).

----------Fundamental Laws and Constitution of New Jersey 1664-1964 (Princeton, Princeton University Press, 1964).

Burnett, Edmund C., ed., Letters of Members of the Continental Congress (Washington, 1921-1936).

Butterfield, L. H., ed., The Adams Papers (Cambridge, Harvard University Press, 1963).

---------- The letters of Benjamin Rush (Princeton, Princeton Univ. Press, 1951).

Cappon, Lester J., ed., The Adams-Jefferson Letters (Chapel Hill, UNC Press, 1959).

Childs, Francis, Printer, Debates and Proceedings of the Constitutional Convention of the State of New York Assembled at Poughkeepsie on the 17th of June, 1788. Facsimile Reprint of an Original Copy by Francis Childs, 1788 (Poughkeepsie, 1905)

Conway, Moncure C., ed., Omitted Chapters of History: Life and Papers of Edmund Randolph (1896).

Cotner, Robert C., Transcriber, <u>Theodore Fosner's Minutes of the Convention at South Kingstown, Rhode Island, 1790</u> (Freeport, New York, 1919. Reprinted 1970).

Cummins, Saxe, ed., <u>Basic Writings of George Washington</u> (New York, 1948).

Elliot, Jonathan, ed., <u>Debates in the Several State Conventions on the Adopting of the Federal Constitution</u> (Philadelphia, 1861)

Fairfield, Roy P., ed., <u>The Federalist Papers</u> (Baltimore, Johns Hopkins Press, 1981).

Farrand, Max, ed., <u>The Records of the Federal Convention of 1787</u> (Yale University Press, 1974).

Force, Peter, ed., <u>American Archives</u> (Washington, 1837-1853)

Ford, Paul L., ed., <u>Essays on the Constitution of the United States, Published During Its Discussion by the People, 1787-1788</u> (Brooklyn, 1892)

----------<u>Pamphlets on the Constitution of the United States Published During Its Discussion by the People</u> (Brooklyn, 1888).

----------<u>The Writings of Thomas Jefferson</u> (New York, Putnam Press, 1892-1899).

----------<u>The Political Writings of John Dickinson</u> (New York, Reprinted 1970).

Handlin, Oscar and Mary, eds., <u>The Popular Sources of Political Authority, Documents on the Massachusetts Constitution of 1780</u> (Cambridge, Harvard Univ. Press, 1966).

Huett, Richard ed., <u>Basic Writings of Thomas Paine</u>, (New York, Willey Book Co., 1942).

Hunt, Gaillard, ed., <u>The Writings of James Madison</u>, (New York, Putnam, 1900-10).

Jensen, Merrill, ed., <u>The Documentary History of the Ratification of the Constitution</u> (Madison, 1976).

Leuchtenberg, William E. and Bernard Wishy, eds., <u>Empire and Nation, Letters from the Federal Farmer, Richard Henry Lee</u> (Englewood Cliffs, Prentice Hall, Inc., 1962).

Lincoln, Charles Z., ed., <u>Messages of the Governors of the State of New York</u> (Albany, 1909).

Lodge, Henry Cabot, ed., <u>The Works of Alexander Hamilton</u>, (New York, G. M. Putnam's Sons, 1904).

McCloskey, Robert Green, ed., <u>James Wilson, Works</u> (Cambridge, 1967).

McIlwaine, H. H., ed., <u>Official Letters of the Governors of the State of Virginia</u> (Richmond, 1926).

McRae, G. J., <u>Life and Correspondence of James Iredell</u>, (New York, 1858).

Morison, Samuel Eliot, ed., <u>Sources & Documents Illustrating the</u>

Selective Bibliography

<u>American Revolution</u> <u>1764-1788</u>, (New York, Oxford University
Press, 1972).
Padover, Saul K., <u>The Complete Madison, His Basic Writings</u> (New
York, Harper and Bros., 1953).
Robertson, David, Comp., <u>Debates and other Proceedings of the
Convention of Virginia</u> (Richmond, 1805).
Saunders, William L., ed., <u>Colonial and State Records of North
Carolina</u> (Raleigh, 1886-1914).
Sparks, Jared, ed., <u>Correspondence of the American Revolution</u>
(Boston, 1853)
Tansill, C. C., ed. <u>Documents Illustrative of the Formation of
the Union of the American States</u>, House Document 398, 69th
Congress (1927).
Taylor, Robert J., ed., <u>Massachusetts Colony to Commonwealth:
Documents on the Formation of its Constitution 1775-1780</u>
(Chapel Hill, UNC Press, 1961).
Thorpe, Francis Newton, ed., <u>The Federal and State Constitutions,
Colonial Charters and Other Organic Laws</u>, (Washington, 1909).
White, William, Printer, <u>Debates and Proceedings in the Conven-
tion of the Commonwealth of Massachusetts, 1786</u> (Boston,
1856).

Introduction

Bailyn, Bernard, <u>Ideological Origins of the American Revolution</u>
(Cambridge, 1967).
Brown, Stuart Gerry, ed., <u>Revolution, Confederation and Constitu-
tion</u> (New York, 1971).
Colburn, H. Trevor, <u>The Lamp of Experience: Whig History and the
Intellectual Origins of the Constitution</u> (Chapel Hill, Press,
1965).
Greene, Jack P., ed., <u>The Reinterpretation of the American Revo-
lution, 1763-1789)</u> (New York, Harper & Row, 1968).
Jensen, Merrill, <u>The New Nation</u>, (New York, Random House, 1950).
Kellenbach, Joseph E., <u>The American Chief Executive, The
Presidency and the Governorship</u> (New York, Harper & Row,
1966).
McDonald, Forest, <u>The Formation of the American Republic 1776-
1790</u> (Boston, 1965.
MacMillan, Margaret B., <u>The War Governors in the American Revolu-
tion,</u> (New York, 1943)
Stevens, C. Ellis, <u>Sources of the Constitution of the United
States,</u> (New York, Macmillan, 1927).
Thach, Charles E. Jr., <u>The Creation of the Presidency 1775-1789</u>
(Baltimore, Johns Hopkins Press, 1966).

177

Selective Bibliography

Warren, Joseph Addison III, <u>Origins of the American Presidency: A
Study in Executive Theory</u>. Unpublished Dissertation. Michigan
University, 1976.

The State Executives

Abbott, W. W., "The Structure of Politics in Georgia: 1782-1789,"
WMQ, 3rd Ser. XIV (1957)

Adams, Willi Paul, <u>The First American Constitutions</u> (Chapel Hill,
UNC Press, 1980).

Alexander, Margaret C., "The Development of the Power of the
State Executive, With Special Reference to the State of New
York," Smith College, <u>Studies in History</u>, II (April, 1917).

Brown, Robert E., <u>Middleclass Democracy and Revolution in Massachusetts 1691-1788,</u> (1955).

Brunhouse, Robert L., <u>The Counter-Revolution in Pennsylvania
1776-1790,</u> (New York, Octagon Books, 1971).

Crowl, Philip A., <u>Maryland During and After the Revolution</u> (Baltimore, 1943).

Daniell, Jere R., <u>Experiment in Republicanism: New Hampshire and
the American Revolution 1741-1794</u> (Cambridge, Harvard Univ.
Press, 1970).

East, R. A., "The Massachusetts Conservatives in the Critical
Period," in Richard B. Morris, ed.,<u>The Era of the American
Revolution</u> (New York, 1939).

Erdman, Charles R. Jr., <u>The New Jersey Constitution of 1776</u>
(Princeton, Princeton Univ. Press, 1929).

Flick, Alexander C., ed., <u>The American Revolution in New York,</u>
(New York, 1967).

Flick, Hugh M., "The Council of Appointment in New York State:
The First Attempt to Regulate Political Patronage, 1777-
1822," <u>New York History Magazine,</u> Vol. 15.

Ford, Paul L., "The Adoption of the Pennsylvania Constitution of
1776", <u>Political Science Quarterly,</u> X (September 1895).

Fowler, William M., <u>The Baron of Beacon Hill. A Biography of John
Hancock,</u> (Boston, 1980).

Gemmill, John K., "The Problems of Power: New Hampshire Government During the Revolution," <u>History of New Hampshire,</u>
(1967), Vol. 22.

Gitterman, J. M., "The Council of Appointment in New York," <u>Poli-
tical Science Quarterly,</u> VII (1892).

Green, Fletcher, <u>Constitutional Development in the South Atlantic
States,</u> (Chapel Hill, UNC Press, 1930).

Hall, Van Beck, <u>Politics Without Parties. Massachusetts 1780-1791</u>
(Pittsburgh, 1972).

Hawke, David, <u>In the Midst of a Revolution</u>, (Philadelphia, 1961).
Hoffman, Ronald A., <u>A Spirit of Dissension: Economics, Politics and the Revolution in Maryland</u> (Baltimore, 1973).
Howe, John R., <u>Changing Political Thought of John Adams</u>, (Princeton Univ. Press, 1966).
Koch, Adrienne, <u>Power, Morals, and the Founding Fathers</u>, (Ithaca, Cornell Univ. Press, 1961).
Lipsom, Leslie, <u>The American Governor from Figurehead to Leader</u>, (Chicago, Univ. of Chicago Press, 1939), 14.
Lockard, Duane, <u>The New Jersey Governor: A Study in Political Power</u> (New Jersey, 1964).
Lundin, Leonard, <u>Cockpit of Revolution: The War for Independence in New Jersey</u> (1940).
McCrary, Edward, <u>History of South Carolina in the Revolution 1775-1780</u>, (New York, 1901)
McCormick, Richard P. <u>Experiment in Independence: New Jersey in the Critical Period 1781-1789</u>, (New Brunswick, 1950).
----------<u>The History of Voting in New Jersey</u> (New Brunswick, 1953)
Main, Jackson Turner, <u>The Sovereign States 1775-1783</u>, (New York, New Viewpoints, 1973).
Mason, Bernard, <u>The Road to Independence: The Revolutionary Movement in New York</u> (Lexington, 1967).
Morison, Samuel Eliot, "The Struggle over the Adoption of the Constitution of Massachusetts, 1780", <u>Proceedings</u>, L (1916-1917).
Morse, John T. Jr., <u>Gouverneur Morris</u>, (New York, 1895).
Munroe, John Z. <u>Federalist Delaware in the Critical Period</u> (New York, 1932).
Nevins, Allan, <u>The American States During and After the Revolution 1775-1789</u>, (New York, 1969).
Peterson, Merrill, ed., <u>Democracy, Liberty, and Property, The State Constitutions of the 1820s</u>, (New York, 1966).
Pole, J. R., <u>Political Representation in England and the Origins of the American Republic</u>, (New York, St. Martin's Press, 1966).
Purcell, Richard J., <u>Connecticut in Transition 1775-1818</u>
Read, H. Clay, "The Delaware Constitution of 1776", <u>Delaware Notes</u>, (1930) VI.
Selsam, Paul J., <u>The Pennsylvania Constitution of 1776: A Study in Revolutionary Democracy</u> (1971).
Spaulding, E. Wilder, <u>His Excellency George Clinton</u>, (New York, 1964).
----------<u>New York in the Critical Period 1783-1789</u> (New York, 1963).

Stevens, W. B., _History of Georgia,_ (Atlanta, 1904-1916).
Street, A. B., _Council of Revision of the State of New York_
    (Albany, 1859).
Sydnor, Charles S., _American Revolutionaries in the Making. Prac-
    tices in Washington's Virginia_ (New York, Macmillan, 1965).
Taylor, Robert J., _Construction of the Massachusetts Constitution_
    (Chapel Hill, Press, 1961).
Upton, Richard F., _Revolutionary New Hampshire_ (New York, 1971).
Webster, William C., "A Comparative Study, _Annals,_ (New York,
    1964).
Williams, John Sharp, _Thomas Jefferson,_ (New York, 1967).
Wood, Gordon S., _The Creation of the American Republic. 1776-1787_
    (New York, W. W. North & Co. Inc., 1969).

The Confederation Executive

Bancroft, George, _History of the Formation of the Constitution of
    the United States of America,_ (New York, 1882).
Bemis, Samuel Flagg, _The Diplomacy of the American Revolution_
    (Bloomington, Univ. Indiana Press, 1967).
Burnett, Edmund Cody, _The Continental Congress,_ (New York, W. W.
    Norton & Co., 1964).
Fisher, Louis, _President and Congress_ (New York, Macmillan,
    1972).
Guggenheim, Jay Caesar, "The Development of Executive Depart-
    ments, in J. Franklin Jameson, ed., _Essays on the Constitu-
    tional History of the United States in the Formative Period
    1775-1789,_ (Freeport, 1970).
Harmon, George D., "The Proposed Amendments to the Articles of
    Confederation," _South Atlantic Quarterly_ (1925).
Henderson, James H., "Constitutionalists and Republicans in the
    Continental Congress, 1776-1786," _Pennsylvania History,_ XXXVI
    (April, 1969).
Jensen, Merrill, _The Articles of Confederation,_ (Madison, 1963).
Learned, Henry P., _The President's Cabinet_ (New Haven, Yale Univ.
    Press, 1912).
Montross, Lynn, _The Reluctant Rebels,_ (New York, Barnes & Noble,
    1970).
Munroe, John J., _Federalist Delaware 1775-1815_ (New Brunswick,
    1954).
Rakove, Jack N., _The Beginnings of National Politics,_ (Baltimore,
    Johns Hopkins Press, 1979).
Sanders, Jennings B., _The Presidency of the Continental Congress
    1774-1789,_ (Gloucester, Mass. 1971).
-----------_Evolution of Executive Departments of the Continental_

Selective Bibliography

Congress 1774-1789 (Chapel Hill, UNC Press, 1935).

Short, Lloyd Milton, The Development of National Administrative Organizations in the United States, (Baltimore, 1923).

Singer, Charles G., South Carolina in the Confederation (Philadelphia, 1941).

Wood, George C., Congressional Control of Foreign Relations During the American Revolution 1774-1789, (Allentown, 1919).

Wriston, Henry M., Executive Agents in American Foreign Relations (Dartmouth, 1929).

The Executive in the Constitutional Convention

Bethea, Andrew J., The Contribution of Charles Pinckney to the Formation of the American Union (Richmond, 1937).

Farrand, Max, The Framing of the Constitution of the United States, (New Haven, Yale Univ. Press, 1974).

Flexner, James Thomas, George Washington and the New Nation: (1783-1793) (Boston, Little, Brown & Co., 1969).

Murphy, William P., The Triumph of Nationalism (Chicago, Quadrangle Books, 1967).

Nott, Charles C., The Mystery of the Pinckney Draught (New York, 1904).

Robinson, Donald L., "The Inventors of the Presidency," Presidential Studies Quarterly, XIII, No. 1.

Rossiter, Clinton, 1787 The Grand Convention (New York, Macmillan Co., 1966).

The Debates

Brandt, Irving, Impeachment (New York, Alfred A. Knopf, 1972).

Corwin, Edward S., The President. Office and Powers. 1787-1984 (New York, NYU Press, 1984).

Levy, Leonard M., ed., The Essays on the Making of the Constitution (New York, 1969).

Long, Breckenridge, Genesis of the Constitution of the United States (New York, 1926).

Merry, Henry J., Constitutional Function of Presidential-Administrative Separation (Washington, 1978)

O'Brien, F. William, "The Executive and the Separation Principle at the Constitutional Convention," Maryland Historical Magazine (September 1960).

Padover, Saul K., To Secure These Blessings: Great Debates of the Constitution (New York, 1962)

Selective Bibliography

Roche, John P., "The Founding Fathers: A Reform Caucus in Action," in Gordon S. Wood, ed., Confederation and Constitution (Boston, Little, Brown & Co., 1973).

Schwartz, Bernard, Commentary on the Constitution of the United States. Powers of the Presidency, (1963).

Ward, Harry M., The Department of War 1781-1795 (Pittsburgh, 1962).

Ratifying the Presidency

Borden, Morton, The Antifederalist Papers (East Lansing, 1965).

De Pauw, Linda G., The Eleventh Pillar (Ithaca, Cornell Univ. Press, 1966).

Josephy, Alvin M. Jr., The Congress of the United States (New York, 1975).

Kenyon, Cecelia M., The Anti-Federalists (Indianapolis, 1966).

Kline, Mary Jo, ed., Alexander Hamilton (New York, 1973).

Koche, Adrienne, Jefferson (Englewood Cliffs, N. J., 1971).

Lewis, John D., Antifederalists Vs. Federalists (San Francisco, 1961)

Leuchtenberg, William E. and Bernard Wishy, eds., Empire and Nation (Englewood Cliffs, Prentice Hall, 1962).

McMaster, John Bach and Frederick D. Stone, Pennsylvania and the Federal Constitution 1787-1788 (Philadelphia, 1942. Reprinted 1970).

Main, Jackson Turner, The Antifederalists (New York, W. W. Norton & Co., 1961).

Miner, Clarence E., Ratification of the Federal Constitution by the State of New York (New York, 1968).

Patterson, Caleb Perry, The Constitutional Principles of Thomas Jefferson (Gloucester, 1967).

Peirce, Neal R., The People's President (New York, Simon & Schuster, 1968.

Schlesinger, Arthur M. Jr., ed., The Coming to Power (New York, Chelsea House, 1972).

Trenholme, Louise Key, The Ratification of the Federal Constitution in North Carolina (New York, 1932).

Tugwell, Rexford, How They Became President (New York, Simon & Schuster, 1964).

Walker, Joseph B., A History of the New Hampshire Convention (Boston, 1888).

Index

Index